Behind the Collar

She Was Caught in a Triangle of Manipulation, Sex and Rejection.

Karen L Dade

Published by Amazon

©2019 by Karen Dade

All rights reserved. This book may not be reproduced in whole or in part, in any form or by any means electronic or mechanical, including photography, recording, or by any information storage and retrieval system now known or hereafter invented, without written permission from the copyright owner.

Graphic Design by: Instagram @monichessart & @tale_graphics

Email the author at Behind.the.collar.55@gmail.com

Or visit the author on the web at:

IamKarenDade.com

Acknowledgments

To my family and extended family, you have been the epitome of what family means. Thank you, and I love you more than words could ever express. You have been the backbone to me in all of this. We've only just begun.

To Chris, even a broken clock is right twice a day. Just kidding. I must get my brother because he is such a joker all the time. You have been great to me while writing this book. I would be remiss if I didn't interject a personal thank you for your insight during this process. Thank you for being a great inspiration and a great brother. Much love.

To Pastor Brandon Jacobs, Lady Vivian Jacobs, and the New Zion Temple family. Where do I start? For your words of encouragement, pushing me, letting me vent, letting me cry, and letting me be who I am, I thank you. Thank you for trusting me and seeing things in me that I didn't see in myself. Pastor, your anointing and integrity speaks volumes. Your teaching and preaching have destroyed yokes and broken major chains off my life. It has been awesome; it ain't over, though. I got Better Coming! I love you both to life.

To Manny, for every word of encouragement, every prayer, every time you listened and did not judge, I love you. You are my second mom forever. God placed you in my life, and I now know why. When I accepted my calling, you were there to guide me even though we had not spoken in years, and now look at our relationship. As I'm blessed, you are blessed. Know this!

To my biggest fan, the gift that God gave me 26 years ago, Minister Ki-Ki. For all the times that I felt like giving up, you were my strength. When I felt empty and unloved, I saw the light in your eyes, and it made me realize what true unrelenting love was. I have watched you grow, and I have seen God's grace over my life in you. You are everything that I wasn't. How awesome God is to allow me to impart things to you that were absent in me. You and God loved me through my hurt. Even though you are my daughter, you are also my strength and my friend. I could not have asked for a better gift than the one God gave me 12/20/92. I thank God for you. You are a preaching machine! There are times I wish my father were here to see you, but I know he's looking down with a smile. You have been blessed with a huge mantel, and you are carrying it well. The third generation of preachers. Wow! I pray that you will stay humble and genuine. I am excited about the road that God has you on as one of his anointed vessels. How beautiful are the feet of those who preach the gospel of peace. Mommy loves you the most!

To the greatest woman I know, Momma, you taught me how to be holy. You taught me how to be strong. You taught me to stand up for and to believe in myself even when others didn't. I know your prayers covered me in the darkest hours of my life. I'm glad that "the prayers of the righteous availeth much." Thank you for nurturing the gifts that were in me the best way you could. You are my heart; always know this!

To my dad, the most brilliant man I have known. Though you are not here, your legacy continues through your children and grandchildren. There were so many times that I had prepared a message and wished that I could run it by you or written a poem and thought about how eloquent you were when you spoke. I have even, at times, sought the qualities that you possess in those that I have loved. Were you perfect? No. But you were my dad, and a huge part of who I am is because of who you were. My heart, at times, bleeds for you, and I pray that I have made you proud. I miss you!

One last, but not final, acknowledgment. I give all thanks and praise to the One who loves me more than I have loved myself. To the One who impregnated me with multiple gifts and talents, allowed them to grow within me, and then birthed them from me; the One responsible for my very being. Every breath I breathe, every step I take, every move I make, every word I say, every thought that echoes in my mind, every beat of my heart I owe it all to Thee. To say thank you is not enough. However, those are the words mortals use to express gratitude. I pray that You, in your infinite wisdom, feel the depth of gratitude for which my words are not adequate enough to speak. To You, I owe it all!

From a daughter to her Father God Almighty.

Contents

Acknowledgments .... - 3 -
Forward by Andria S. Hudson .... - 10 -
Introduction .... - 12 -
The Exordium: In the Beginning .... - 17 -
The Experience: How it Unfolded .... - 25 -
    Act I – Scene I .... - 29 -
    Scene II .... - 36 -
The Exposition: Trying to Bring Some Clarity .... - 39 -
    Act II – Scene I .... - 39 -
    Scene II .... - 42 -
    Scene III .... - 43 -
    Scene IV .... - 46 -
    Scene V .... - 48 -
    Scene VI .... - 50 -
    Scene VII .... - 53 -
    Scene VIII .... - 56 -
    Scene IV .... - 57 -
The Entanglement: Getting Caught in the Trap .... - 66 -
    ACT III – Scene I .... - 70 -
    Scene II .... - 71 -
The Ebbing: Drifting Further from the Truth .... - 74 -
    ACT IV – Scene I .... - 76 -
    Scene II .... - 78 -

The Enslavement: In a State of Dependency/Addiction	- 85 -
Act V – Scene I	- 95 -
Scene II	- 96 -
Scene III	- 97 -
Scene IV	- 97 -
Scene V	- 100 -
Scene VI	- 104 -
The Emancipation: Got Free but Can't Get Right	- 111 -
The Evolution: Starting to Progress	- 116 -
Act VI - Scene I	- 123 -
Scene II	- 129 -
Scene III	- 133 -
The Enlightenment: The Darkness Uncovered	- 135 -
The Exhortation: My Appeal	- 141 -
The Election: Oh, To Be Chosen	- 150 -
The Exordium: Beginning Again	- 160 -
The Exultation: Welcome to My Beginning	- 167 -
The Extremity: The Wrap Up	- 175 -
For Your Entertainment: Expressions for your pleasure	- 181 -
I Am Not the One	- 181 -
You Just Don't Understand	- 184 -
Not a Good Place to Be!	- 186 -
The Last Refrain	- 189 -
Who Knew?	- 192 -
Broken I Am	- 195 -

Pain	- 197 -
Independence Day	- 200 -
Yet Again	- 203 -
Amend	- 205 -
Tired!	- 208 -
To Thee	- 210 -
"I Never Knew" (Original song lyrics)	- 213 -
No Longer Waiting to Exhale	- 215 -
Out of All of This, God, You Get the Glory!	- 218 -
Dedication: Ode to Kiki	- 222 -
What I Want / What I Need	- 225 -
When	- 227 -

Forward by Andria S. Hudson

Serving in a ministerial capacity does not exempt one from trauma, tragedy, hurt, or even betrayal. In fact, ministry is an attractive magnet for such life experiences. With elevation and promotion of any kind comes warfare.

Jesus instructed us in his word in John 16:33 (CEV): "I have told you this, so that you might have peace in your hearts because of me. While you are in the world, you will have to suffer. But cheer up! I have defeated the world." One does not bypass trouble, yet he or she has the power through Jesus Christ to overcome trouble and become a living testimony of the power of grace.

When life hurts, how do you deal? When life abandons, how do you cope?

When life victimizes you, how do you find purpose in the pain?

Your testimony was created by God to empower the world. It's almost oxymoronic that pain has the potential to yield goodness. Conquering life's battles was never designed to be stories that get buried in ashes and rubbles of resentment but to emerge with beauty to show that one can not only survive but thrive!

Behind the Collar is a riveting autobiography of grace, freedom, restoration, and forgiveness. Karen Dade's descriptive, yet hilarious, banter will provoke you to every emotion possible-anger, disbelief, sadness, and ultimately joy. Dade proves that behind every achievement, there is an expensive price to be paid. *Behind the Collar* is an eye opener for parents, teens, leaders, ministers, and of course women.

I applaud Minister Karen for her decision to be unashamed of and unapologetic for her triumphant story. Her life has not at all been easy, but it has been worth it. In fact, that's what life is really all about; it is about revealing our stories for victory and not for misery.

We can expect more outstanding things from this amazing author as she continues to fulfill her destiny and what she has been created to do on this earth.

What is behind YOUR story?

Andria S. Hudson

Introduction

Triangle: a situation involving three people or things, especially an emotional relationship involving a couple and a third person with whom one of them is involved. Manipulation, sex, and rejection formed the underlying triangle of my life. These three nouns have been abysmal in almost every situation with every person I have encountered. The terms have engulfed and surrounded me as I reflect on my life. Unbeknownst to me, I was caught in a vicious series with myself as the main character. This is not a role that I would have chosen because it's paradoxical. Even so, it will trigger and spark curiosity to all who read my narrative.

I began this journey seeking answers to questions about my life, and the lives of too many other people while praying for guidance and wisdom to share with you. In my pursuit, I examine those who have been called to preach, pastor, and minister, like myself. As one chosen by God to preach His Word, having answered His call in 2002, and preached my first sermon in 2003, I am, nonetheless, emboldened by what I have learned through a painful and wrenching examination of my life. That's why I feel purposed to tell you my story; because it, in many ways, mirrors so many other lives, filled with the lowest of emotional and physical valleys, as well as, apexes of emotional and physical mountains of joy and fulfillment. Until I examined myself and became transparent before God and to myself, I could not answer the questions about the life I had lived. Much less the reasons so many others do not live the lives of fullness and abundance that we are all capable of living, even though we have been predestined to do so.

So, here is my life, with all its vicissitudes and adversities, many brought on by myself, as well as the great moments of enlightenment, edification, understanding, and awareness that guide me to this day.

I used a plethora of adjectives writing this book. I also laughed (because every life must have some levity in it). I cried, I praised, and I worshipped, not necessarily in that order, throughout the discovery and writing process. As you enter in and take this journey with me, hopefully, you will experience the same gamut of emotions that I did, and perhaps relate to many of them.

I've heard it said that everyone has a story, and I believe that is true. If I didn't believe with all my heart that my story might help you and others get delivered and set free, I would not waste time telling it. "The good, the bad, and the ugly" about my life that I disclose in this book are composite experiences that have brought me to where I am today. They are the threads that comprise my life's tapestry, which continues to expand in my witness and my testimony. I intended to be as real, as raw and as graphic in the telling of my story to you as I had to be to myself and before God, who, of course, already knew it all, but was waiting for me to come before Him in full repentance with truthful confession. Only then could I be healed and emancipated of my past so that I could go on to the future He planned for me.

This book is not for the faint of heart; it may not be suitable or appealing to people of a certain age. Thus, I offer a disclaimer that it's explicit and at times, X-rated. Again, I am laying it all out before you. Be prepared for its realistic and honest account. I do not describe my life as I do for shock value, or to create a riveting read. Rather, I tell you "the whole truth and nothing but the truth," which I deviate from only to safeguard certain confidentialities. It is unequivocally clear to me that part of my ministry involves telling my story to reach those who have had similar experiences, so they may know that God is a deliverer and they can go from being a victim to a victor! I know that it has only been through God's power and might that I have survived a hellish past, that I, indeed, have overcome, and that others too, including you, can be triumphant and unbound from the past or present allurements, enticements, and fascinations that seduce you and capture you in their snares repeatedly.

It's my sincere prayer that this book is a contrivance and a vehicle for some in their journey to God. I titled the book "Behind the Collar" because it was my journey to my destiny as not just a preacher of the gospel but to my freedom. I lived in chains and enslavement for so long and had no idea that I even needed a release. I had a penthouse suite in hell physically, mentally, and emotionally. Can't tell me to go to hell. Been there, done that! Next!

The collar can be used as a metaphor for what your struggle was or is on the way to fulfilling your purpose and to answering the call on your life. We walk around as if we are okay, with the façade of Christianity, but we are so far from it, and that is not okay. Things can lie dormant for years, but it takes only one seemingly insignificant word, thought, or action to awaken them again. I desire that if you haven't, you will have your awakening and begin the road to restoration.

Throughout the book, you will see excerpts from, "Poems from the Heart," which is my next book. These poems are not frivolous or random entries. Rather, they are indicative of what I was experiencing emotionally but expressed poetically. So, do not dismiss them. They will take you deeper, giving you greater insight into my state of mind and heart.

Now, let the journey commence.

1

The Exordium: In the Beginning

I was born December 2, 1963, at Chicago Lyon Inn Hospital to the late Dr. Tommie J. Jr. & Ursula I. Dade. My mom said that I was like a baby doll. I was ebullient all the time, singing and dancing. She named me Karen.

Karen: Danish form of Katherine, a cognate of the Greek Aikaterine, the root of which is katharos (pure, unsullied).

Hmm, the evil irony of this. The enemy knew that the meaning of my name would not hold for most of my life because of a set of circumstances inflicted upon me.

I have three siblings, Tommie III, Katrice, and Christopher Dade. We were "PK's," preacher's kids, and, as such, we were as far from perfect as any other kids. I was born and raised in the church. My father was a preacher/pastor of Beacon Hill Missionary Baptist Church. He became a pastor when I was seven years old. I remember singing with my best friend Sudana when we sat with the congregation. We sang so loud and knew all the songs so well that we joined the adult choir between the ages of eight and nine years old. I directed my first song, "We Are the Salt of the Earth," at the tender age of thirteen.

In 1982, my father became ill and retired from pastoring. He passed away in 1989. My family joined New Covenant Baptist Church in 1985 when I was twenty-two years old. I was highly active with the young adult choir and became one of the choir directors. My family moved to East Chicago, Indiana, where I joined St. Mark African Methodist Episcopal Zion Church at the age of twenty-seven. I became a director and teacher of the youth choir under Macbeth Harris. My brother, Tommie Dade III, then became the Minister of Music at New Hope Missionary Baptist Church, of Hammond, Indiana, and I followed him there. I eventually became the choir director and teacher over the youth, adult, and Mass Choirs. While under Pastor Herman A. Polk, I accepted my calling into the ministry. I was there for eleven years, and in October 2009, I joined New Zion Temple under then-Elder, but now-Bishop Brandon A. Jacobs. I became an ordained elder in 2013, and I am currently a member of the ministerial staff. To God, be the glory!

My life was anything but idyllic, just as most lives aren't. Being raised in church does not mean that I lived a holy life. Indeed, the opposite is true.

My mother was, and still is, a beautiful woman. She has a fair complexion, high cheekbones, as like a Native American with Asian eyes, bob wig, (it's an Afro now), five foot three, and she is quite shapely and surprisingly strong. She is now ninety, but the years have been kind to her. She doesn't look a day over sixty. She has always had a certain je ne sais quoi about her. Many call her jazzy and sophisticated; I call her my beautiful mom.

Mom was creative. As I reflect, I see her tending to her summer vegetable garden every year and pickling mostly cucumbers. Those homemade pickles were "wassup"! (This is slang for "what's up" or "the bomb" meaning "very good"). She did needlepoint usually making something for the house, or to wear. It looked painstaking and tedious, but she enjoyed it, so it mattered not the tiresome hours she invested. Once, she made a blouse from scratch with no sewing machine. She's an accomplished soloist, and her voice, even today, has an eloquence and purity that I pray I have at her age. Mom decorated her behind off long before everyone thought of "Martha Stewart" as the expert interior decorator. Her house was always immaculate, never out of sorts, and she accomplished this work dutifully at home while serving as the church Sunday School Superintendent, program maker on a carbon copy typewriter and using stencils, finance clerk, and whatever else my dad needed her to do. Plus, she made sure all her children had what they needed for school. She even worked part-time as an educator in the school system. Chaka Khan sang, I'm Every Woman, but my mother outperformed the woman in that song immeasurably. I don't know how she did it all.

My mom and I were estranged, even though we lived in the same house. We never had conversations. She said it; I did it, or succumbed to the gauntlet, literally. She was a disciplinarian in every sense of the word. She didn't play. When she proclaimed anything to us, she was animated and hyper; this reflected her normal disposition. The only time she reached a real place of tranquility, was while accomplishing a task. With all that was on her plate, trying to balance it was a major feat. I hadn't thought of it that way until now. As a child, you rarely think about how your parents provide for you, or all that they do to keep things afloat. Mom and I never saw eye-to-eye. If she saw powder blue, I saw navy blue. If she tasted lemon, I tasted lime. This is how it was for years, even into adulthood.

God has brought my mom, and I closer now. Most importantly, she was there when I needed her the most. The good thing about God and life is that if He gives you life, you can better your life. Although she never said, "I love you" while I was growing up, she makes up for it now. Thank God for grace. We all need it. She tells me often that she loves me. Better late than never! She was and still is, there when I need her. She is my rock, and I see her now for the strong, black, holy woman she is. We still sometimes don't see eye to eye, but we do see closer shades of blue.

My daddy was fair-skinned, almost white, with black curly hair, five foot eleven, and thin. He was *fine*. He was a child prodigy, -a straight "A" student from grammar school through college. He had a doctorate in Theology. He was inducted into the "Who's Who of Preachers," and he was a great expositor. My daddy exposed a message like no other. He was brilliant but reserved, and sort of a recluse. It's hard to believe that as outgoing as he had to be as a preacher/pastor, he was the exact opposite at home. He had a quaintness about him. He loved to tell jokes, and when he was tickled, he'd turn beet red.

Daddy desired anything mentally stimulating and challenging. He was always working the crossword puzzles in the newspaper. Those were the hardest puzzles, but he completed them without access to the internet. He was a master word connoisseur. I guess that's where I got it. I had a closer relationship with him than my siblings did. My dad and I were television show buddies. We watched Magnum P.I., Beretta, Hawaii Five-O, Mannix, The Rockford Files, and the Chicago Cubs baseball team. We watched baseball religiously. I can hear him calling me now, "Karen, the Cubs are on." I'd yell back, "Okay, Daddy, I'm coming." Man, I loved those moments with my dad. I cried like a baby when the Cubs finally won, just wishing dad were here to see it.

I used to taunt my father a lot, though. I picked at him until he turned red, and that irritated him to the point that he would yell, "Sit down somewhere ole stupid gal!"

Hilarious! My father never hit me, though. Low key, I was his favorite, but don't tell my siblings. Those were good times, and I miss him.

Ironically, the closeness that defined my relationship with my dad mirrored how distant we were at the same time. My father was responsible for my humor, wit, and brilliance but also for my ignorance about relationships. He challenged me by indulging me in battles of the mind. He would say something, and then challenge me to top it. It was a game he devised, and one that we played vigorously; at times for hours. However, we didn't have real conversations. Neither my mother or father armed me with information about how to conduct myself as a young lady, or how a man should treat me. I never saw my mother and father embrace, nor did I hear them tell each other, "I love you." They never snuggled, flirted, or teased each other. There were times that they would bop. (Old school dance). Everything else was all about ministry. That is a huge area of dysfunction in marriages with pastors, their wives, and their children. You can't be, so ministry-minded that you neglect to build a relationship with your wife and children. I see why my mother felt somewhat empty. She longed for what women naturally desire, the warmth of a man. Not just the physical touch, the mental stimulation, and the spiritual connection, or what some call chemistry. My father loved me. He expressed it by spending time with me and telling me how proud he was of my academic achievements, but I never heard the words or felt the warm embrace. I never felt it from either of my parents. That was why it was easy for me to fall prey to the predator; because, subconsciously, I was longing for the affection that I wasn't getting or the love from a man that I needed, or maybe I just longed for a physical experience altogether. I know this is why I hugged and kissed my daughter so much, once I was blessed to have her. I didn't want her to crave for something that I could freely give her. I lived and learned. Unfortunately, I did it the hard way.

2

The Experience: How it Unfolded

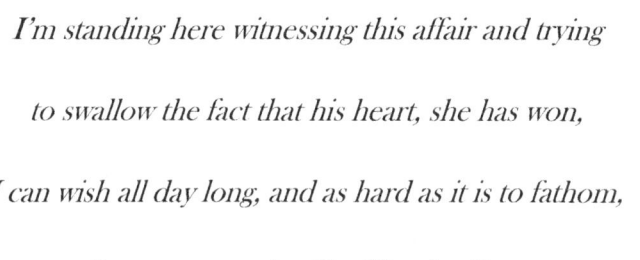

I'm standing here witnessing this affair and trying

to swallow the fact that his heart, she has won,

I can wish all day long, and as hard as it is to fathom,

I must accept that I'm Not the One.

My mother was like a sentinel watching over her children. We were not allowed to hang out with many people, go over to friends' houses, or participate in sleepovers. The only people I could hang with were my sister and brother. I had a little pink record player. I recall playing the forty-five by K.C. & the Sunshine Band entitled, "Shake Your Booty," and my mother forbade it. Boy, have times changed!

Again, my brother was a musician, so he had a lot of musician friends. One was Todd Dandridge, who was, and is a very accomplished musician, singer, and songwriter. He was a chocolate brother. He wasn't the most attractive person physically, but he was a musician and a singer, and in church, that's almost like being a preacher. Being a singer in a church is like having celebrity status. Plus, he was older than me. He was twenty at the time. I was eleven years old; I became infatuated with him, as a lot of young girls do with older males. I always wanted to be with my brother when I knew Todd was around. He was my brother's best friend at the time and close to our family. I grew increasingly fonder of him, and he became increasingly fonder of me. My fixation was normal; his, of course, was inappropriate.

I was a child, and he was a grown man who seemed old beyond his years. Todd hung around those who were much older, and my brother was no exception. My brother is twelve years my senior. Also, Todd had been the minister-of-music at his father's church and composed music for others for years. Understand that being eleven in 1974 was like being eight today. The media and the internet have quite a bit of influence over the growth of our children today. The maturity levels and what they are exposed to; there is a huge disparity from back when I was a child. I was book smart but had no street savvy.

Even considering the times, my parents sheltered me. I never had the, "What's inappropriate?" conversation. There were no obscenities in records, and no overly explicit lyrics, except in the Underground. No videos displaying half-naked, gyrating women were playing. I was not permitted to watch R-rated movies. Talk about green. It could have been the pigment of my skin.

Let's be clear, though, and it's not the child's responsibility to be an adult and exhibit adult behavior; it's the adult's responsibility to be an adult. It's not abnormal for a young girl to be bright-eyed and bushy-tailed over an older guy. How often in most young girl's and boy's lives are their crushes on a coach, teacher, or celebrity? What's abnormal is an adult acting on the crush.

For example, I had a crush on Peabo Bryson and just knew we would do duets together and get married. It was what I fantasized about.

I can affirm that the molestation damaged and changed my entire life forever. God healed the fragmented pieces of my heart, mind, and soul, but it takes time. Some women never recover, and those of us that do, still never forget.

Molestation is disgusting, deplorable, debasing, demoralizing, demonic, and demented. The perpetrators should be locked up along with several others, but God will avenge.

As I reflected on my life to write this book, it was like looking at a movie in which I was the star of the show. As I got into the meat of the story, I found myself structuring each chapter in my life, like acts or scenes in a movie or play.

"Ladies and Gentlemen, please take your seats because our feature presentation is about to begin!"

When I was twelve years old, and in the eighth grade, I was tiny. My body filled out when I turned thirty, and my daughter arrived. I was teased in eighth grade because I only weighed 101 lbs. When I finally developed some breasts mid-year, they accused me of stuffing my bra. They gave me the nickname "Cush.".". Kids can be cruel.

Act I – Scene I

Now let's get back to Todd. He fascinated me, and he knew it. He flirted with me. I felt like I had McDonald's, i.e., I'm loving it! I liked him! My first kiss happened in the kitchen of my brother's place. Todd came close to me, causing butterflies in my stomach. I got warmer as he got closer, and he kissed me. Wow! That's wassup! It's my first kiss, and I don't know how to do it. I kissed with my mouth open, and Todd instructed me how to do it correctly. I was a quick learner, so once was enough for me to perfect it. My brother was in the other room. When he returned, we quickly adjusted, and he had no clue. Why would he even think his friend was making out with his eleven- year- old sister? My infatuation for Todd increased.

We talked all the time. I snuck phone calls to him. My parents were oblivious to what was occurring right under their noses. I don't blame them, though. One thing about being a female, we learn how to be sneaky and cunning early. It's part of our DNA. We made arrangements to see each other. The phone thing was good, but we talked as if we are girlfriend and boyfriend and now it's time to date. I imagined that I was entering a full-blown relationship. That is the normal line of progression.

He picked me up every day from grammar school. At first, it was maybe once or twice a week, but it quickly turned into an everyday occurrence. He picked me up from school and drove to some remote place. We lived in a new development where there were several plots of undeveloped land that provided privacy, so a hiding place wasn't hard to find. He must have done some investigating first because we went right there without any hesitation. He parked, and we talked, but only for a moment. I had to be home at least by four o'clock. The intimacy began during these meetings. There was never any penile penetration, so perhaps that is why he felt feel okay about it all.

He fondled my breasts, kissed me, and penetrated me with his fingers. I felt his fingers going deeper and deeper inside of me, rubbing, and touching every wall. He reached the labia as he massaged my clitoris. I became wetter and wetter to the point where I soaked his seats, flowing like a river.

My body was surging and experiencing minor convulsions. I released myself to enjoy and absorb every moment. Everything was free and easy, and time paused. My mind, body, and soul became encased in a whirlwind of unexplainable and unimaginable feelings that became ineluctable. I connected to him, and tears flowed down my face. These tears are different, though. I wasn't sad; I was happy, but in an entirely different way than when I felt happy from riding my bike or playing with my dolls. I had no real comprehension of the encounter. I experienced ecstasy and felt euphoric. I had an out of body experience. I saw and felt everything. Every kiss and every touch took me higher and higher into this place of no return and relentless joy. We were touching each other. He fondled me until I had my first orgasmic experience. My entire body tensed and then relaxed. I thought, Oh my goodness! I have never, ever, ever, EVER, felt anything remotely as good as this! What the what? My body was shaking. My mind was swirling in circles. It was surreal - like I was there, but not there. There was a sense of peace and calm that came over me. I was sleepy, and I needed something to eat.

My first orgasm was with my first love. He withdrew his fingers from me, and I saw the fruits of my love dripping incessantly down his fingers. He wiped them on a towel that he had in the back seat. He kissed me gently. The best kiss I had ever had. My life couldn't have been more perfect. He started the car and drove me to the corner of my street. We kissed again, and I skipped home. I was satiated and in love. It was ecstasy, but it would later turn into a place of torment, despair, and sorrow.

Why was I having orgasms at the age of now twelve? I still rode my bike through the neighborhood. I played jacks, hopscotch, and double-dutch. I built my barbie dream house out of books. I had an adolescent mind and life, but I had to deal with adult emotions and situations.

I went from liking him to feeling what I believed and perceived as love. We engaged in sexual activity daily for my entire eighth grade school year. I spiritually, mentally, emotionally, and physically connected to this man. My commitment and love for him were bewitching. They were as deep as love could be between a male and a female. In my mind, I created a life for us that would be our couple of forevers. I thought about him every day, all day, dreaming about and craving him. I was like a dope fiend on crack. In school, I incessantly watched the clock because three o'clock couldn't come fast enough. I got to see my lover. As three o'clock approached, the butterflies in my stomach increased. My heart palpitations quickened, like labor pains.

I was salivating, hungry, and thirsty as if I was about to attend a smorgasbord that featured all my favorite dishes. I didn't understand it all, but I didn't care. It felt amazing, and I was in love. I talked to him more and more. I sang to him and dedicated my favorite song by Switch to him, "They'll Never Be a Better Love." My mind, heart, and soul were consumed by him every waking moment. I was a young girl who had not even reached puberty, but my body responded as if I were already a woman!

Then something devastating happened. He told me that he was getting married.

What the heck? Getting married? Did I miss something? Am I dreaming? Okay, in a minute, I will wake up. "How can this be?" I was hysterical.

He tried to calm me and make me understand. I was twelve, and the reasoning part of my brain would not fully develop until twenty-five. I cried for days on end. He still spent time with me, but the visits become more and more infrequent until they ended. After all, he was getting married.

Eventually, when three o'clock approached, there was no him, no me, no us. I wanted him, but I couldn't have him. He made a promise to another. I didn't understand it at all. At now thirteen, I experienced the worst, most god-awful pain. I should not have been there. I was a kid, but in an adult scenario.

He tried to make me understand that even though there was an "us," there could never be an "us." Huh? Wait! What? What? I wanted to die. I was dead on the inside. I was an empty shell of a girl, with womanly woes.

He appeared to feel bad about it, but if he felt so bad, why was he doing this to me? Now I understand why I'm so private. My brother always told me that I never tell anyone anything, and I don't talk. I learned at an early age how to hide my emotions and keep things to myself. Darn it; I should have been an actress. This is a gift! Why didn't he shoot me? How was I going to survive?

The wedding day arrived. It felt like a bulldozer had dumped a bunch of gravel on me because every part of my body ached. After all, we shared, I thought he loved me. I was supposed to be his wife. I was totally confused. I told him that I was going to object at the wedding, but I knew I wouldn't, and he knew I wouldn't. I listened as he sang to her while she walked down the aisle in her long white gown. I was crying buckets on the inside, but I couldn't show it. I hurt so badly but I couldn't express it. The whole time I imagined that she was me, and I was her. The song he sang was, "God Sent Me an Angel." My chest felt as if it was going to explode or implode. The pain was colossal. I remember it vividly, even now.

Every step she took toward a new life with him was also a step toward what felt like my demise. I was dying inside, and I couldn't tell a soul! I knew of God, but I didn't know Him. I mean, I went to church, but I hadn't built a relationship with Him yet, so I had to travel the road alone. I didn't know to call on Him to help and guide me through that network of debauchery, despair, and dismay. This was my first encounter with real pain and rejection. For a long time, feeling rejected was the overwhelming theme in my life, and it defined my behavior with men.

I wished I could click my heels three times and replace the bride. I wished I had won his heart.

Scene II

Next on the scene, was Antonio Levy, my piano and vocal teacher. I was fifteen. He was twenty-nine. He was another one of my brother's friends. That place felt familiar, but sadly, I was immune to it. You know, the older guy and young girl scenario. My heart was cold and dark. Being emotionless was not good for a teenager. What was to be my plight? I was emotionally numb, which is never good; but it was what it was. He was twenty-nine, tall, light caramel latte, wavy black hair, and an angelic voice. Mmmmmm! And he was married. Pause! Married? Yes. Married!

I took lessons at my dad's church every week. He was also close to my family. If only they'd known there was unseemly behavior taking place in the church house.

He was giving me a lesson and leaned over to kiss me. He took my hand and placed it on his genitalia. We left the sanctuary and went into the foyer. I guess he had a little conscience. I fondled him until he had an orgasm. That didn't occur too many times, but it added another scar, nonetheless. I didn't even like him like that. He wasn't Todd, so whatever.

End Scene

Some may wonder why I didn't stop such behavior or know that it was wrong. Understand that I trusted those people, and, in my case, I built a wall. As mentioned previously, I had become emotionally numb, frozen, deadened, and detached. My behavior felt like an act. I felt like I had a part in a play. Other than that, I didn't know why I was doing it. I had no emotional attachment at all to Mr. Levy. I submitted to people and situations. My naiveté was my downfall. For whatever reason, such encounters didn't feel wrong. That was because I felt nothing at all. The first experience threw me into a traumatic detachment. No one taught me to avoid such scenarios, and I didn't know that they were forbidden. We didn't talk about such subjects back in my day. The discipline was not built on open and honest conversations in the family structure. The modus operandi was "do what I say. The end!" Discussions of sex and sexuality were taboo.

Those men were and are pedophiles, and that is the bottom line. If you judge me for my role in our encounters, that's your prerogative; you cannot judge me. God's agape love is wonderful, and it allows me to walk in freedom. It allowed me to stop beating myself up and saved me from drowning in my guilt. I have been healed. I pray and hope my story will bring others to know God's unconditional love as well. The problems that I face now are the lust and sexual demons that haunt and taunt me. If I could have chosen another path, believe me, I would have. Then again, had I taken another path, I would not have my story to share with those who need to hear it. I couldn't share how God took what the devil meant for bad and turned it for my good. He can do the same for you if you allow Him to.

3

The Exposition: Trying to Bring Some Clarity

If I love the way I do, inevitably,

the pain is here to stay.

Stay as a reminder of what I never

want to feel again,

That is the pain, which can only come, from

putting your trust and faith in a man.

The foundation was laid, and the stage set for my life to unfold. Unravel is a better depiction. I chased the feeling I had with Todd.

Act II – Scene I

At nineteen, I was singing in and directing the choir when I met Pastor David Matthews. He was about fifteen years my senior, but we liked each other. We had a sexual affair. I figured we were both single so that it couldn't be wrong. Well, other than that he was a pastor and we were Christians, nothing was wrong. He lived in the South part of Indiana, about three hours away, so it was easy to keep the relationship a secret. We visited each other off and on for about a year. The sex was boring. He was non-emotional and disconnected. For me, the attraction wasn't about the sex; I was drawn to him because he was an older man. Plus, he was a pastor, and he was single, so I imagined myself as "First Lady." I imagined it, but it was never my desire. When I was young, I watched my mother and saw all she went through. I vowed I'd steer clear of such a role. If you're unfamiliar with the African American church, "First Lady" is the title we bestow on the wives of the pastors of our churches. Women have purposed themselves to believe that the title of "First Lady" is some glorified title and position without understanding that it's more than big hats, bauble-beaded suits, and church anniversaries. I didn't want that role. It's more than what you see on the surface. If you want to know more, and you don't know anyone that's a

"First Lady," there are several books on it, and then there is always Google.

With Pastor David Matthews and me, no such thing would occur. I didn't like him like that either. Our affair was just something to do. I was in it, though, and perhaps it could've led to something permanent and meaningful, but I had no expectations. Well, that's what I told myself. He told me that he wasn't ready to get married. We stopped seeing each other, and then he got married. The truth was, he didn't want to marry me. How could he marry someone else? I went to visit him, gave him my goodies, and spent my money to see him. I had issues. Low self-esteem reared its ugly head. What was wrong with me? Rejection! Why did it keep happening to me? I was baffled.

Even though I didn't care for him, I thought, how dare he not choose me. Funny thing, though, I wasn't hurt at that time. I had a bruised ego, but otherwise, it was whatever. The wall and barrier that I had built held up was strong. It was mostly about sex. He was an older man, and what I was accustomed to so, I felt I could keep him if sex were part of the equation. The crazy part, as I said, was that it wasn't even good sex. He was well endowed, but it was like having sex with a corpse.

Scene II

My first real relationship was with Colvin McDuffy. It was a perfect relationship. We had met at the bowling alley, and instantly, our eyes had locked. We shared our first kiss that night. He was sexy, tall, lean, and chocolate. I was twenty, and I had met my best friend and true love. The problem was, I was so emotionally scarred that I didn't even know he was the real deal. We entered a year-long relationship. We did everything together; we never argued. We were friends and lovers. He was such a good man. He was the best I'd had in every way.

I'm now fifty-five, and I have yet to meet another who was as good as he was. He once told me that I was his best, as well.

Time passed, and I became pregnant. Me, the pastor's daughter. I can't plead ignorance in this instance. Unprotected sex can lead to pregnancy. What was I going to do? I deliberated over it and concluded that I was not ready to be a mother. Additionally, I was the pastor's daughter, and my sister had already gotten pregnant before marriage. So, I had an abortion. My sister was the only one that knew. She tried to talk to me and make sure that it was the course I was willing to take. She liked Colvin, and she saw he was a good man, even at his age. Colvin and I talked to a mother figure in his life, and she explained how we could get married and be a family. Blah, blah, blah. I didn't hear any of that. A mother and wife at twenty-one? "Buzz." Wrong answer! He was willing to step up and do the right thing. I wasn't.

I still hadn't allowed myself to feel. The things from my past had penetrated me so intensely, I found myself running from them completely or capitulating too deeply. I had gone from one extreme to the other.

My abortion devastated him. I even taunted him about it. He cried because I was going to kill his child. I, of course, apologized for my behavior, but why did I even do that to him? What type of monster had I become? He loved me, and I couldn't see it. I'll get back to this later.

Scene III

During my relationship with Colvin, I met Louis C. Halibut, who would be my future "Baby Daddy." He was an older man. Well, to me, he was, even though there was only a five-year difference in our ages. I was attracted to older men. The number of years was not significant. I wanted the Todd feeling back again. I believe this was the only reason I acceded to being with him in the first place because of desensitization.

He was attractive, had a good job, and a nice car, but I was in a relationship with Colvin. I broke up with Colvin to be with Louis. He called me to find out why. He even called my sister, looking for answers. I ended up talking to his sister-in-law, and she tried to convince me to think it over, but not me - not Karen. I had it all figured out. I wanted Louis. I wish I could go back, slap, and punch myself in my throat!

I began dating Louis at twenty years old. Twelve years I spent off and on with him in this merry-go-round of commotion. Up today and down today. I dated others; he dated others, and it was a hot boiling mess. It went from mental to verbal to physical abuse. The physical started as a tug here and a snatch there and then heightened into something bigger.

I started talking to him and became convinced that this man would be better for me based on what was superficial versus anything substantial. Colvin tried and tried to get back together. He does not understand why I ended our perfect relationship, and to tell you the truth, I didn't know either. I did know that I hurt him, and the thought of it now brings tears to my eyes. I often wonder if the pain that I have experienced in every relationship afterward is my penance for the hurt I caused him so profoundly. Leaving him and transitioning into the relationship with Louis was a huge mistake. Huge mistake!

Let me state here, emphatically, that I love the product of our relationship - our daughter Kianna, and I wouldn't change that to save my life. But the marriage thing, well, it never should have been. In retrospect, we never should've dated.

While dating, it was an extremely volatile relationship. We argued every day, day, and night. My mother told me, "Anytime you argue with someone every day, that is an indication that it's not a good, healthy relationship." Did I listen? Of course not! Who listens to their mother? The whole situation was hellish. He would break up with me because he felt like it, and I would consistently take him back. There were countless times that I cried profusely because he was evil to me. He was evil incarnate. He was Satan's spawn. He was Satan's brother. I know they must be related. He had penetrated the walls and barriers around my emotions. I began to feel, but my feelings returned for the wrong person and at the wrong time.

That time in my life affected me so gravely that I, once again, see it as a movie that could surely be about someone else's life. But no, it was my life. And the drama continued.

Scene IV
Early in our relationship, Louis picked me up, and we went to his house; well, it was his momma and daddy's house. We got into an argument, as usual, and I told him to take me home. He refused. He told me to find my way home, and he left, but he left his car there. I was angry, and I wanted to get even. The wheels are "a-turning." I went outside and found the sharpest rock I could find. I etched

in his windshield, "I Hate You." I made it as big and as deep as I could. I covered the entire windshield of his nice, black, shiny sports car. I took my little, happy, self-back into the house, had a seat on the couch, and whistled until he returned. He got back and was surprised that I was still there. How was I supposed to get home when he brought me there? I mentioned to his father that he refused to take me home, and he expressed dismay. Louis had not yet seen his car. He went back out and noticed the inscription in the windshield. He stormed back into the house. He was furious. I was fine because he should've taken me home. He told his father what I did, and his father told him, "You should've taken the girl home." I concurred. He drove around for weeks with his windshield like that. Co-workers saw it. Friends saw it, and I saw it each time I went out. But we stayed together. That was wrong, but it illustrated how explosive our relationship was. This, unfortunately, was the beginning of all that was wrong on so many levels.

It was early in our relationship. The mental and physical abuse got deeper.

He had a close friend named Zeke. They did everything together, but mostly they drank. Had I not experienced enough darkness? It kept getting worse. It was one of the worst nights of my life.

Scene V

One night, we had sex, and he turned to me and said that he wanted me to sleep with his friend. I was, of course, avidly against this idea; but he said, "If you love me, you'll do it. I want to watch it. I will be there the entire time." I started crying because it was not something I wanted to do at all, but I had opened myself up to him, and we were connected. For whatever reason, I can't say NO.

Some women don't understand how deep "soul ties" are. A "soul tie" is a deeply felt emotion about another person that they can't imagine living without him/her, even though that person may be treating them badly. Soul ties are no joke, and we must be careful to whom we allow ourselves to be connected. I wish there had been someone who would have explained to me how detrimental and dissolute such a relationship would be, but no one did. No one did! Then again, would I have even listened?

Louis described to me how this torrid act would play out. I would be facing him the entire time, and Zeke would enter. I would never have to see him. He would penetrate me from behind. He talked me into it. He already had control over me, so I must submit and do what he says. Up until this moment, there had been subtle bouts of physical abuse, but they would escalate. I thought I loved him, but he did not love me. This dark and despicable act tore me to the core of my soul. Would a man that loves me even consider this? Pimp me out to his friend? He pimped me out to his friend! I was his property. He was my pimp, and I was his whore. It is the most degrading and disparaging thing that a man can do to a woman.

I heard the door open as Zeke entered. I didn't see him, but I heard him. I was crying before it even happened. I was on my knees when he penetrated me, with Louis lying underneath me. It didn't last long, but it seemed like forever. As it ended, and I heard him leave, I felt his semen drip from me like a slow leaking faucet. I felt like a bitch for real. What made me agree to this? I can't even imagine, but there I was, and here it is. I was there trying not to think about what happened to me. How do I wrap my mind around this? How do I recover from this? I felt dirty, nasty, filthy, and wretched. Louis saw the pain and anguish on my face. He was apologetic for subjecting me to it, but I was damaged.

Scene VI

We were on vacation in Jamaica, and out at the local club enjoying that island feel and music. In Jamaica, it's all about the mood. He, of course, became intoxicated. I never recognized how heavy a drinker he was, because we didn't go clubbing together, and he never drank around me; so, it wasn't obvious. That night should have made me run fast, but instead, I stayed slow, literally.

I went to our room to take a shower. Unbeknownst to me, he followed me shortly after that. I didn't hear him knock on the hotel door because, again, I was in the shower. When I got out, I heard the hotel assistant let him in. We only had one room key. He shut the door, grabbed me, slammed me to the floor, and gave me a black eye. My eye was swollen shut. I'm glad that we were on vacation. So, I had a couple of days to get the swelling down. He was afraid that I might retaliate, so he slept on the balcony. I awakened to talk about what had just happened. He heard me and jumped on alert. I guess he thought I might try to hurt him. The last thing either of us desired was to be in jail in Jamaica. We talked and then had sex. The relationship was a lust thing. I realize that what we had didn't consist of the elements of love. We never had anything in common except we both liked to eat. That does not make for a good friendship, let alone a good relationship, and not grounds for a good marriage.

I was lying on my back with the ice pack on my eye, as he pleasured himself at my expense. What am I doing? I vowed I would never be that woman. The one portrayed in the movies. He beats her, then apologizes and makes love to her battered and bruised body. But I was her; she was me. How did I end up in this theatrical production? I saw the script, read the storyline, but I don't recall ever auditioning for the role or accepting it. Somehow, I was thrown into it and was the lead actress. The only difference was, I wished it were an act, but wasn't. Just ask my eye.

I got home and made up this elaborate story about why my eye is black and blue. "See what had happened was, I was in the water on the beach. Then I stumbled and fell and hit my eye on a rock." I sold it, and some bought it. There were skeptics, but no one dared to cross me. I had a mouth, and I was persuasive.

We continued to date, but not without warning. I always warned him. I declared to him that if he ever hit me again, it would not end pretty. I reflected on what I had with Colvin, my first love. My relationship was on a fast climb to nowhere. I got in touch with Colvin and tried my best to get back with him. I tried to sex him to death. But, mentally and emotionally, he was gone. I hurt him, and nothing else mattered. All trust in me was gone. I thought my body was my weapon. He had to come back; I'm the "bomb diggity" in bed. I got mad skills, so he said. The point was, I knew that he loved me. I hurt him and betrayed his trust. It was all I knew to do. It was a conditioned behavior, but I don't know that yet. I mean, hurt and betrayal was what was done to me, so it was only normal to inflict it back. Right?

The girl that Colvin started dating after me was the one he married and is still married to today. I found out that he is overly possessive and paranoid about her leaving him. He never had children. I feel I'm partially responsible for him behaving this way because I caused him devastation and nearly irreparable damage. I wish I could apologize; (Lord, please forgive me, please).

Scene VII

Louis and I had one more bout with physical abuse before we were married and I lost my mind, literally.

We rode in the car and argued, per usual. He was driving, and he grabbed me by my collar. I went into a rage. My mind focused on an incident that occurred with my sister. She was in a physically abusive relationship when I was eight. Her husband almost killed her. Her face swelled to the point that I didn't recognize her. I thought at that moment, "Awe hell.... Naw!" That black eye thing will not happen again! Or what happened to my sister.

I took my hand and dug my nails into the side of Louis' face so far that I saw the white meat. I had exceedingly long acrylic nails. (I'm more demure now). Then I took my right leg, kicked him in the head, and his head hit the window. He was driving, but all I thought was, this ends now and today! This was Tina and Ike Turner stuff! "Lord, help me!" In a nutshell, we never crossed that bridge again.

Sidebar: *I would never advocate that this was the best solution. However, no one deserves to be abused by a man under any circumstances. Most men that abuse women are cowards, and the last thing they want is a woman that can or will fight back. If you are in an abusive relationship, get out. It's not worth your life!*

My younger brother is the militant of my two brothers. I often wonder if he had been older, and come to my rescue, how the story would have ended, thank goodness that:

"All things work together for the good of them that love God, to them that are the called according to his purpose." (Romans 8:28)

After the on and off relationship and abuse with Louis, I discovered I was pregnant. When I told him, he was elated and insisted that we get married. We had a wedding. I mean, we got married. If things are not right before, they will not be right after.

The wedding day arrived. Oh, happy day, happy, happy. I'm walking down the aisle, and he was bawling like a baby. What the hell? I'm not over-exaggerating. He cried as if someone had died. While we were on our honeymoon, he mentioned to another couple that he had cried at our wedding. They asked him why. He said because he thought about how badly he had treated me, and I was so beautiful when he saw me.

We were scheduled to go to Cancun in the morning after the ceremony, but we didn't even spend our wedding night together. He left and went drinking with his friends. I went along with the flow. My mom was upset about that.

She said, "Who leaves their bride and goes out drinking on their wedding night?" She was angry, but it mattered not. Why? "Cuz, I'z married now." (Art certainly imitates life. The character, "Shug" in the movie, The Color Purple, who wanted her estranged preacher father's approval so badly that she yelled that to him as he passed by her in a carriage – "I'z married now!")

Sidebar: *Marriage is more than doves, flower arrangements, bridesmaids, and a flower girl with cute pigtails. If dating is* *bad, the marriage will be worse. Everything good gets better, and everything bad gets worse. It all becomes magnified. It is serious and not to be entered lightly. The enemy hates anything that God ordains, and we, as Christians, need to understand the severity of it and stop acting like marriage is a lunch choice from a menu that you can send back if you don't like it. It's easy as Heaven to get in but hard as Hell to get out!*

We were married, new house, new baby. She was the joy of my life, Kianna. She looked like a Hawaiian baby doll, simply beautiful. A few months into our marriage, he decided he did not want to come home one night. Here we go.

Scene VIII

One afternoon he left for work. He was on 2nd shift, three pm to eleven pm. Eleven o'clock rolled around. He called me and told me he was going out for a drink. At eight am the next morning, he was not home. I dropped off Ki-Ki (Kianna's nickname) and went to work. Hot as a recently fired pistol, I drove to work. He eventually called around nine am. I couldn't discuss it because I was at work. Once I got home, it was on and popping like popcorn. (I know that was corny).

The excuse he gave was that he was drinking, it got late, and he decided to spend the night at his friend's house. Hmmm.

My response, "Okay, you were drinking, and you got so drunk that you couldn't come home, and you couldn't call?" (Lord, help my disbelief). I wondered, "*have I married an alcoholic or a straight idiot?*" I was not a drinker. There were occasions where I had a Daiquiri or a Slow Gin Fizz, but most would say that it is like having fruit punch. After the huge argument that ricocheted off that ridiculous story, I concluded that he thought I was stupid.

However, I had no real proof that he was lying so, I told him, "This is your first and final warning."

He had an encore performance. He didn't heed the warning.

Scene IV
One bright and sunny morning after Louis had neither come home all night nor called me again; I heard Luther singing: Sun a-shining, there's plenty of life. A new day is

dawning, sunny, and bright. (remix) I'm about to lose my baby. I'm about to lose my baby.

I was at work, and it was noon. Thirteen hours had passed, and Louis and I hadn't communicated. We were married! I was at my window cubicle in the office, looking out over the city, and the phone rang.

"Hello."

"Hey, Babe." He stated.

"Heeeeey." In my calm voice.

"What you doing?"

"Well, considering that you called me at work, I'm working."

"You mad?"

"Should I be mad?"

"Well, see what happened..."

I cut him off.

"You know what? I'm at work now, so I'll talk to

you when I get home, okay?"

"Okay."

"Bye-bye." I hung up the phone.

My calm demeanor had confused him. He had no way of knowing how to take me. I had the power, and I was in control. I got home, told him I was leaving and called my brother to come and get me.

He was irate and started throwing all my shoes down the stairs screaming, "If you want to leave, leave!"

By this time, I had accumulated over 500 pairs of shoes. You can only imagine if I had that many shoes than shoes were my thing, my passion! I witnessed each pair as they tumbled out of their respective containers onto the steps and the floor. I was furious! As each pair hit the floor, I became more irate. My blood was boiling. I didn't know what else to do, so I called his mother. I knew he would listen to her. Well, I thought he would. I got her on the phone and told her what was happening. She told me to put him on the phone. At first, he wouldn't respond, but eventually, he came down the stairs, kicking and stepping on my shoes, crushing the boxes, and stomping on them. Grrrrrrr. As he approached me, I bust him in the cheek with the receiver. A little blood trickled out. I hit him kind of hard.

He threatened, "I should tell the police."

I responded, "Tell them."

I was pissed off! My brother got there with huge bags for my shoes. He looked at Louis and shook his head. Louis screamed at him, telling him not to shake his head at him. He was right. My brother should have bitch-slapped his sorry ass because he was acting like a bitch. (Excuse the language) It was how I felt at the time. I called the police. They came and removed him so that I could gather my things.

I was separated, with a one-year-old baby. I could and would not raise my daughter, pretending that it was a real marriage! He wanted to act single, so single he should be.

End Scene

Here is a little more about Louis before we close this chapter. I was on bed rest with my daughter in the early stages of my pregnancy. It was the most miserable time of my life. Again, Louis and I argued all the time, and he was mean as a junkyard dog. That didn't change because I was pregnant. I cried so much while carrying her that I'm surprised she wasn't a fussy baby. The only thing that saved me was my family. They were my place of refuge and kept me laughing all the time. We are a crazy family, and when we are together, it's Comedy Central at its finest. I was on bed rest because I was spotting. I wasn't supposed to do anything. I had a huge argument with Louis. I hung up the phone and ran to the park. I swung on the swing extremely hard and sobbed. I hoped that I miscarried. I didn't want to be pregnant or have his child. At eight months pregnant, I would get on my knees, lean over, and clean the tub so that I could take a bath because he wouldn't clean it after himself. I am glad God didn't grant my prayer to take my child. I cannot imagine my life without Kianna.

Louis was an excellent source of income, but horrible concerning the emotional and spiritual side of her growth. I felt that it was my fault because I chose him, and my daughter paid for that decision. As a small child, he behaved as a loving father should, but as she progressed to her adolescent and teenage years, things changed. He hates me to this day. It's amazing how people have issues with a person that *they* wronged. After twenty-six years, he's still not over it. Why he is still harboring emotion and bitterness that long is beyond me. His bitterness showed a diminished mental capacity to reason. I had to console her countless times because he cursed her out, called her some horrible name, or devalued her altogether.

Things like, "You will probably be nothing and end up pregnant," or "I wish I never had you." One time, specifically, when she was about sixteen, I told her that the best thing she could do was to pray for him.

She said, "I'm tired of praying for him."

I responded, "You must consider the source. When a person does not have a relationship with God, they will say and do anything."

No Holy Ghost, no control! A father is vital to the development of a child. For females, often, it determines the type of men we choose and what we tolerate in relationships. I remember praying when my daughter was small that God would give me what I needed to be a mother and a father in those areas. I wouldn't have had to do it, though, if I had chosen wisely in the first place. I am grateful that God allowed me to build her up in those places that he tried to break her down. God is so awesome. I have a wonderful daughter. She hasn't been perfect, but she's a very anointed preacher and grammar schoolteacher. I am a proud mother!

Sidebar: *Please be cognizant of whom you choose to father your children. This is important. We often, sleep with these men and don't take into account that they could end up fathering our children. Then we get mad when they turn out to be deadbeat fathers. They are typically deadbeat men, so what else could they be as a father? Check out the fabric before you choose to wear the outfit! Remember, you are connected forever to this person, and it's the children who ultimately suffer. The proper way, of course, is to have children within the holy union of marriage. This choice should be made wisely, as well. Children deserve to have a decent mother and father. Also, we need to stop saying that* *our pregnancies were mistakes when we choose whether we are going to get pregnant. We control our bodies. We choose the method of birth control. Are there exceptions to the rule, where a woman is using birth control, and she still becomes pregnant? Yes, but they are not in the majority. We either get caught up in the moment, or we don't shield ourselves as we should. Exercise wisdom in all things, especially when a life is involved!*

I hope that some men read this book and it brings clarity regarding some things about women, because, clearly, there are some things that men "Just Don't understand."

While I was transitioning from that situation, I met Ethan Milgram. Not yet divorced but moving on. Look, you can't start one thing without ending another. Even when one is not faithful to you, you still must be faithful. We were separated but separated is not divorced. You must completely end one thing and give yourself time to heal before proceeding to something else. If not, you carry baggage. (Sing, Erykah Badu, sing your "Bag Lady" song.)

I can't be alone, though. I can't be alone. That is what I told myself. I hadn't given myself time to examine my behavior or heal. I'm using the relationship with Ethan as a means of rebounding, but I'm going in reverse.

So, I was with Ethan and filing for divorce. While dating Ethan, I met Colby Banniker. Lord have mercy!

4

The Entanglement: Getting Caught in the Trap

"Oh, what a tangled web we weave..."- Sir Walter Scott

I met Ethan through a mutual friend. He was a nice-looking guy; brown complexion, nice height, and build. He was a bit of a drinker, and I knew it, but it didn't bother me. I had an inkling early on that we would probably not get married. He was a cheapskate. He lived in the basement of his parents' house so he wouldn't have to pay to live on his own. Now mind you, he could afford to be on his own. I mean really could afford it. All his family confirmed that he was good at handling money and was well off.

Sidebar: *For those who may not know, any grown, non-disabled man should not be living at home with his parents* *in his thirties. Periodt! The only exception is if he is taking care of his sick parents. He also should not be living off **you**!*

I met Colby, one day when I visited the beauty shop in October 1995. I spotted a chocolate, tall, smooth, debonair barber working there. I had never seen him there before, so I asked who he was. His name was Colby Banneker. He was put together well. My beautician told me some of his story. He was a widow with a four-year-old daughter, dabbled in real estate, and was five years my senior. I was thirty-two at the time. He fit the Karen profile. So, naturally, I flirted with him. He flirted back. He told me not to get involved with him because he was addictive.

My ego kicked in, and I responded, "Ditto." By 1996, we got involved. Meanwhile, "living-at-home-with-his-parents." Ethan was still in the picture. I was the player, or so I thought. When you play, you always get played. That went on until December of 1996 when I get busted. Ethan found out about Colby and me, and he dumped me.

I begged and begged for him to stay with me. He didn't hear any of that foolishness. I cheated, and I deserved to be dumped. The crazy part was, he wasn't right for me anyway. He was controlling and bossy.

He would say things to me like, "What did I say?" or "Didn't I tell you....." I was a mess without a clue. I was walking around with my eyes wide shut!

I was dating Ethan and Colby. Colby was dating Deirdre and me. So instead of a triangle, it was a rectangle of lust and deceit. The devil will make a fool out of you if you let him. How did I get so far off the beaten path? I was a church girl, active in the church, singing and directing. Nobody would have imagined. After this book, there will be no more guesswork. The devil thought he had me, but God! I got loosed here. In yo face Satan! I'm so glad that I'm saved and set free because I was on my way straight to hell, first-class, and on the express flight! Whew, Jesus! Thank You, Jesus!

Ethan dumped me, but I continued dating Colby. I was in love with him, but it wasn't a healthy love.

Colby and I had this incredible sexual chemistry that transcended all normality. It was hypnotic, exotic, neurotic, and psychotic. Psychotic because I had convinced myself that it was real love with real substance, but it was all predicated upon lies, deceit, and control. We both loved to dance and made love countless times on the dance floor when we would go stepping. People would watch us because we moved and communicated so well non-verbally. It was all in the dance, and that buildup of kinetic energy transferred and flowed like a wave from the dance floor straight to the bedroom. I mean, it was always rhythmic, like a well-composed nocturne. When we touched and made love, it was sensual and explosive. Every time was like the first time. It was never regimented and always felt new.

Colby is the first man, as a grown woman, that made me feel like I had an out-of-body experience. The orgasmic experience brought me to tears on several occasions. This was like when I was a teenager. I had finally found and achieved that feeling, what I had been missing, so I thought. The emotional connection was dreamlike. There were times I tried not to cry, but for whatever reason, the tears were uncontrollable. I am sure this played a paramount role in why I could not disconnect from him. He was right. He was ad(dick)tive. (We are grown here.)

The relationship status went from rectangular to triangular. It was Colby, Dierdre, and me. I had convinced myself that eventually, he would leave her and be with me. I dated him exclusively for a whole year. One whole year and my relationship status never changed.

Sidebar: *Ladies, if you are dating a guy and he never acknowledges you as anything other than his friend, Uh, Duh, that is all you are! Period, exclamation point! Stop hanging around acting like a girlfriend and a wife, doing things like a girlfriend and a wife, while in his mind, you are not even close to being either one.*

I was the chick on the side. The web was getting bigger.

ACT III - Scene I

I was pregnant. Colvin told me that if I didn't' have an abortion, there was no chance of us ever being anything. I loved him so, my dumb self listened to him, and I was on the abortion table, again. The first time didn't affect me emotionally, but that time messed me up for sure. Why would I even listen to him? He was a bully, and I let him bully me into murder. He told me he would pay half the cost. I should have seen who he was by this, but caught up in love, I was. I was depressed because I didn't want to go through with the abortion. I felt connected to this child. The first time was not a big deal to me because I was emotionally dead, but now that I had opened my heart, I could feel him/her growing inside of me.

Scene II

Abortion day: They took me through a series of questioning and a video. They wanted me to be sure that I was cognizant of what was about to happen and to ensure I was clear about what I was doing.

I laid there on that table, and the technician asked, "Are you ready?"

I responded, "Yes."

But, on the inside, I'm screaming, "N-o-o-o-o!" I wanted to tell her that I don't want to do it. I wish she could've read my thoughts. If only she would've engaged me in conversation, but it was not her job to counsel me. She had one purpose and one purpose only, and that was to suck the life out of me.

She turned and flipped a switch, and this loud machine turns on. I saw her grab the long thin nozzle of the vacuum cleaner. Before she put it inside of me, she explained that I would feel some pulling and discomfort, but nothing worse than a cramp. What she didn't know, was that emotionally, I was already feeling and experiencing pain more excruciating than a cramp. My legs were in the stirrups, the sheet over me when the nozzle entered. She inserted it inside of me as I listened to the machine, suck the life out of me, literally. With every tug, pull, and pinch, my soul died. The tears were streaming down my face. Oh my God, my child! The king or queen that was destined to be here. I'm a murderer. I had killed my baby because a man told me to. The abortion was a low point in my life. I was devastated and destroyed. I went home, balled up in my bed, and cried myself to sleep. How, God, do I rebound from this? My seed, my seed, how could I? God, please forgive me and take away the pain, please!

The control, the low self-esteem, and the timorousness of rejection were all evident and laid bare before me, but I couldn't see it. Yes, low self-esteem. That was funny. Because I always carried myself outwardly as if I was "the stuff," not arrogant, but extremely confident. That was the exterior shell, but all the underlying layers were scarred, torn, shredded, and chewed up.

Then he started dating Dierdre, Sheila, and me. I had had enough. I was done. So done you could stick a fort in me.

5

The Ebbing: Drifting Further from the Truth

Remove these chains of bondage, Lord; I want to again be free.

Free to feel, free to dance, free to love and be one in the institution you have decreed for humanity,

But right now, where I am is Not a Good Place to Be!

I was like a ship without a sail. How did I drift so far from my morals? How had I abandoned and excluded the principles that I knew to be right? It's as if they were eradicated from my mind and my soul. Again, I had been in church all my life, but obviously, the church was not in me.

A family member introduced me to Denzel Corporal. She thought that since he was single and I was single, we would make a good pair. That was so far from the truth. He wasn't what I typically liked. How many times was I going to press replay on this same video? Geez! He had a light complexion, and I preferred dark men. I decided to try something different. He was shorter than I liked, and he was a Seventh Day Adventist. What the hell am I doing now? That was the beginning of the drift. He was also about ten years my senior. It had become an endless pattern.

ACT IV - Scene I

We began dating in June of 1999 and became engaged by September of the same year. We planned to marry in December of 1999. That was our plan, but not God's plan. Thank you, Jesus! I was in the process of buying a home, so we decided we would move in together, you know, seeing that we were going to get married. I decided to shack, on the premise that we were going to get married. I knew better, but I did what I wanted to do. As usual!

We moved into the house in November, and all hell broke loose. I mean *all hell*! All that could go wrong went wrong. He was very controlling, what a surprise.

I stopped going to my church and went with him on Saturdays at his church. I tried to make the transition and conversion to become a Seventh Day Adventist. I feel like I'm having an out-of-body experience again because I don't recognize this person at all. All these out-of-body experiences... What am I, an astral projector? Writing this book has me in some form of a paranormal anomaly like feature.

Then, he got his private phone line! He informed me that I couldn't use it or answer it. I complied with Denzel's request. I heard him on the phone talking low or in code. I was a good little shacker. He got off the phone and had to leave on business, so he consistently avowed. He told me he wanted more kids. I stopped taking my pills because I was trying to get pregnant, hoping that would solidify our relationship and act as a bond between us. I had convinced myself that if I had a baby, everything would be all right.

As if producing a baby was like going to the pound and choosing a puppy. "Aw honey, that one is cute, we will name it Sparky." It's a life; a human being, not a pet.

Sidebar: *Quit using these precious gifts from God as pawns. Having a child is not a game. A child is a person that you are responsible for nurturing, guiding, and providing a healthy environment to ensure that he/she can grow up and be a productive member of society. Having a baby does not make a relationship better. In a relationship that is already bad, having a baby only adds insult to injury. If the relationship is a mess, a baby added to the mess is "a baby added to mess."*

I found out that he was still married. He, of course, lied to me and told me that he was divorced, but supposedly something had happened, and the dog ate the paperwork, and his fingers broke, and the house caught on fire. Yadda, yadda, yadda, I was a fornicator/shacker/adulterer. Pure foolishness!

Scene II

One night, my family and I decided to go out to dinner to celebrate a birthday. While we were there, who shows up with some woman? Denzel. My family unanimously decided they were going to jump her and him, but I managed to settle them down. In retrospect, we should've beat the brakes off them both. Well at least off of him. She started to say something to me, and I quickly informed her that the wisest thing for her to do was keep silent. She complied. What a wise little trollop she was. She had to be about ten. I am facetious, of course. I was young, and she was about ten years younger than me. He made up an elaborate story. My family told me I needed to leave with them.

I said, "No."

I wasn't involved with the church much by now. Our relationship ended dramatically. There was a huge argument, he pushed me, and the cops were involved. He was a police officer, so he decided to call them to protect him and me. (I was talking to my mother about this scenario, as I was writing this book, and she reminded to me how I was crying and crying, pleading with Denzel to stay with me. My God, I have no recollection of this. There are some things better forgotten. However, I needed to recall these pieces to the puzzle of my life for such a time as this. I needed to man up or woman up. Well, something up!) I have seen him since then with "Miss Little House on the Prairie." They were married and had two children. I must say they were the cutest kids. Oh, well.

When I look back on it all, there were several feelings involved there, and I swept through the entire gamut of them. There was embarrassment, I had given up my entire identity for this man and situation, and that was where I ended up? My mother warned me, but in my stubbornness, I didn't listen. There were the signs and red flags that I should have used mere common sense to discern, but I allowed them all to fly past me. I was angry, sad, ashamed, distraught, depressed, etc. It was obvious to everyone but me. I didn't see the pattern of behavior and self-destructive habits I had developed in my relationships with men. I was experiencing the same disappointments, and the result was typically the same. I had blinders on, and through the scales, I couldn't see, but one thing is unequivocally clear, it was Not a Good Place to Be!

"When I look back over my life, and I think things over. I can say that I've been blessed; I've Got A Testimony" --- of how God is a sentry for babies and fools. I was without a doubt on the fools' boat - in the front, paddling "...far from the distant shore, very deeply stained within and sinking to rise no more, waiting for the Master to rescue me." Of course, he wasn't going to rescue me because I didn't have sense enough yet to make a despairing cry. God, please save me from me!

We didn't disconnect, even during that blowup and the breakup. I forgot to mention that he co-signed on the house so we could get a better rate. It was all my money for the down payment, though. I asked him to sign the house over to me, and he told me I had to buy him out. The devil! I was stressed. Why? Had I not been through enough? Who could I blame, though, but for me? Again, mom told me that my decision to move in with him in the first place wasn't one approved by God but, who listens to their mother?

She always said, "A hard head leaves a soft behind." She tried to appeal to him as a self-proclaimed man of God. God will never bless mess. Believe that, especially when there is a calling on your life and even more so if God chooses you. I had a calling when I was in my twenties, but at that time, as you've probably figured out, I wasn't trying to be a preacher, date a preacher, or marry one. Ironically, God decided to make me one. Real funny, Lord. Real funny.

After Denzel, I become a member of New Hope Baptist Church, and I tried to get back on track. I ended up in a state of depression. The enemy was trying to kill my daughter and me. He knew the destiny of our lives, so why not kill two birds with one stone?

I'm glad that God loved me enough to stay near, because if it weren't for Him and my daughter, I wouldn't be here.

Wouldn't Be Here (Original Song Lyrics)

I remember driving home in my car, feeling beaten down, battered, tattered, and worn.

I remember driving home in my car, baby in the back seat, but I still felt all alone.

Pulled up to the garage, thought to myself, I can't take it no more.

Grabbed the remote to the garage before I knew it, I had shut the door.

Sat there for a while, don't know how long, didn't

know which way to turn.

All I can tell you right now is for death, oh, I did yearn.

Suddenly, I felt her hand,

She touched me from the backseat' cause she didn't understand.

Right then God broke the spell in my mind and said, "Karen you can make it,

Yes, you can!"

If it wasn't for you, I know I Wouldn't Be Here!

I've made some mistakes I wish I didn't make,

I've been in some places that made my heart ache,

I've even said some things that I wish I didn't say,

But because of God's grace, I'm still

here today.

If it wasn't for you, I know I Wouldn't Be Here!

If God had not used my daughter to break the spell that was in my mind, I would've killed both of us by Carbon Monoxide poisoning by sitting there in that closed garage with the car running. Excuse me while I take a praise break.

I was praying and asking God now for forgiveness, and to help me with the house situation. We are good until things get out of control. Then we cry, "Oh, Lord..." Ridiculous! What would we do if we didn't have the Lord to rescue us from ourselves? Good thing He is faithful even when we are not.

"If we are faithless, He remains faithful, for He cannot deny Himself." (2 Timothy 2:13 NASB)

I was crying over my breakup with Denzel and the confrontation about the house so much that it even carried over at work.

One day, my co-worker, Angela Childress, pulled me to the side, "You have to get it together. The people at work don't need to know that you are having a problem. Pray on it, and let it go."

That wasn't an easy task, but the more I did it, the better things became. I eventually stopped worrying about it. I had to go on living my life. A few weeks passed, and I got a phone call from Denzel. He told me that he was applying for some secret service job, and his name couldn't be on the house. Then, he quick-claimed the property to me. Thank you, God, for saving me from myself. *Again*!

Denzel and I were over, and Colby re-entered the scene. Colby, the smooth operator that bullied me into the abortion. Yeah! Him!

6

The Enslavement: In a State of Dependency/Addiction

Each second, each moment, and each day

that passes, my love will tell,

Just know that I'm here for you in every way, no matter what it entails.

Be my love forever, and forever my love will remain,

Even until the end of time and when the music reaches its

Last Refrain.

"If the Son, therefore, shall make you free, ye shall be free indeed." (John 8:36 KJV)

If you want to be free. There are times when one can be so bound that they can't see that they are in shackles. I had developed a serious "soul tie" with Colby. How many times was I going to end up on the rat's wheel? I was going in circles, spinning my wheels. No, Karen, don't go back. I sometimes wish I was a "looper," so I could loop myself into the past and slap myself before I made another asinine decision. Several times I wanted to slap and punch myself in the gut.

We dated and broke up repeatedly. He dumped me, and I dumped him. The same man that told me we would never be anything unless I had an abortion.

That lasted until September 2003. We broke up. I had finally accepted my calling in 2002, and my conscience wouldn't let me play this game anymore. We had played the back and forth thing for ten years. I had to get it together.

The relationship between Colby and me was melodramatic. After I accepted my calling in 2002, I was clear about the path I would take. We parted ways for what I thought to be the last time. For the first time in my life, I was single, celibate, and loving it.

Then I met Elder Reynard Tolliver. That didn't last long because I was stuck on stupid - (Colby). My heartstrings attached like a puppet to Colby.

While preparing to preach my initial sermon, I saw a commercial about abortion stating how life begins as early as conception. I had been praying to God to show me myself. If you ask it, you better be prepared to see the good, the bad, and the ugly. For me, the ugly was the abortions. I realized that I had not completely repented for them or released the pain. I saw the commercial, and it hit me like a ton of bricks. It felt like someone took a stake and drove it through my heart.

I cried and yelled, *"What have I done? What have I done? Oh, God, what have I done?"*

I fell to my knees and cried for hours, begging, and begging for God's forgiveness. I felt like David when he cried out to the Lord to save the son that Bathsheba had borne. I experienced a superfluity of mental highs and lows, but the most demoralizing was that I had not taken the gift of life seriously. I made a selfish choice to abort those babies. Who did I think I was? What right did I have?

But I serve a forgiving, merciful, and gracious God. After repenting, He said that He forgave me, but it was hard for me to forgive myself. I felt so unworthy to walk in this calling.

One of the biggest issues we have as believers is that we can't get over what God has already forgiven. If He can get over it, surely, we can! We keep reminding God of things that he has long forgotten. If you are truly repentant for what you've done, He is faithful and just to forgive.

"If we confess our sins, he is faithful and just to forgive us our sins, and to cleanse us from all unrighteousness." (I John 1:9 KJV)

God also states that he will throw our sins in the sea of forgetfulness.

"I, even I, am he that blotteth out thy transgressions for mine own sake and will not remember thy sins. (Isaiah 43:25 KJV)

Once you repent, (In my Italian mafia accent), Forget about it! God has forgiven, and He has forgotten. Thank you, Lord, for your grace.

I preached my initial sermon on January 2003, and I have my first solo concert in June of the same year. Things were going well!

September 2003. Colby calls. (Run, Karen, Run. Darn it!) I answered. We talk and talk and talk. We discuss all the past hurt, betrayal, lies, and decide we would get back together, again. I made it clear that if we got back together, we were getting married. He agreed.

December of 2003. I will never forget that day. It was flu season, I was at work, and I couldn't get warm. I was walking around the office with my fur coat on shivering. I had the flu. I was praying all the way home. I had developed a bad case of the shakes. I remembered my grandmother telling me about hot toddies. I stopped at the liquor store and purchased a little bottle of whiskey. I didn't care who saw me or what they thought. I had to break my fever. I got home, made the toddy, and went straight to bed. Colby arrived at my house sometime that evening. I was out of it. He walked in and showed me the ring, but I'm so stricken with fever, I couldn't even see. I lifted my head to acknowledge him and went back into my feverish stupor. Perhaps this should have been a sign.

I recovered, and plans proceeded. The man that I had been pining over for ten years was finally about to become my husband. The New Year was approaching, and all things were becoming new. Never thought that day would come, but it had arrived.

Who Knew?

In anticipation of the marriage and the move to his house, I had a huge garage sale. I sold almost everything. He got the proceeds from all that I sold because he was doing some renovations on (his) house, and I was contributing.

I had purchased a two-flat building in 1999. I used all my hard-earned money to do it. I was so proud of that investment. More about this later.

Sidebar: *If you are going to move into their home, you had better get your name put on the house, or the best solution, the two of you get a new house together. Not everyone is honorable and willing to do what is fair and equitable. "If" things crumble, you will be without anything; because the* *house is in their name, especially if the years that you have invested are minimal.*

My fiancé was very well to do. He was a real estate lender, meaning, he loaned his own money to those who don't have enough funds at closing. He had been retired from his corporate career since the age of thirty-six. He had a daughter two years older than Ki-Ki and was a widow. He had been a single father, until then.

July 3, 2004, rolled around, and it was our wedding day. Beautiful day, beautiful wedding, and the beautiful honeymoon in Cancun to come, or so I thought. Man, I had found my soul mate and felt like the Kenny Loggins' song, "This Is It." I know I'm dating myself. Whatever! I wrote a poem for him and recorded it in my voice to play on the recorder, but the recorder never played. I sang "You Bring Out the Best in Me," by Vanessa Bell Armstrong to him. I was elated. I was such a beautiful bride. Hey, it was my wedding. My colors were gold and emerald green. I was the belle of the ball, the queen about to marry her king. I got ready in anticipation of things to come and the new journey ahead. I felt that I could relax and enjoy the rest of my life.

I dedicated my life to be his wife. I stood and declared my vows:

There was a time in my life that I felt I really knew what it was to be loved by a man and to be truly in love with a man. I felt that all I could possibly ever want and desire, I had found. I felt like I was unstoppable, impenetrable as though I had reached the pinnacle of the true essence of life, love, and freedom, but then came you.

You have shown me a love so gentle and kind and warm that it must be from a higher source than you. In my high-spiritedness, your voice and your touch calm me and allows me to relax, knowing that you have my best interest at heart, and you deserve my humility.

Know this day amongst all that are here in witness, that I'm your missing rib! Our minds and soon our souls and spirits will be forever bonded and connected. God has made us whole and complete in Him and has, therefore, made us ready to become one. I'm here, to, in every way, be your helpmate. I will, always, be supportive of you and help you to meet your goals and ambitions. I will fulfill every desire and satisfy your every yearning.

Divorce is not an option, for we know how to kneel and pray, and seek direction from on high. When the time comes that we must have a life without the other, it will be in death, and our vows will have been fulfilled. Our marriage will be a ministry. We will define the true meaning of marriage, and we will be the example for all to see. Our daughters will observe how a man is when he loves a woman as Christ loves His bride, the church, and they will see through me how to be submissive to a true man of God. So, I, Karen Lynez Dade, on this day, declare myself as your queen and you, my king, and unto God and thee I submit and commit unto you, and you only, my undying love. For even unto death, my love is eternal. So, I vow to be your lifelong companion, forever being by your side, until when my last breath is taken, and with God, my spirit will then abide.

Blah, blah, blah, yadda, yadda, yadda, etc.

That is what I thought it was going to be like for me. I believed that was my forever. How was I so blind to all that was going on? Again, if you start off messy, nine times out of ten, it will end the same way. I don't know what happened, but it wasn't heaven at all. It was the beginning of another realm or crevice of hell.

When Ki-Ki and I first arrived on the scene, my stepdaughter Raynise was resentful of us, as any child would. But I was a woman of God, and that was what prevailed and eased her resentment. I treated her as if she were mine. Where I went, she and Ki-Ki went. When I moved, they moved, just like that. She was emotionally damaged and scarred. I nicknamed her "Weeping Willow" because she would cry even when laughing. She wasn't accustomed to laughing and being silly like Ki-Ki and me. I tried to convince Colby that she needed and wanted counseling. She had lost her mother, and lived with him, heck, I needed counseling. He wouldn't hear of it, so I prayed that God would give me what I needed to be a mother for her, and He is so wonderful that He did. Raynise went to church, and Hallelujah got saved. I preached at her baptism service. Even though her dad's and my relationship was crap, I praised God for our relationship and for the soul that was won.

Act V – Scene I

We were in Cancun getting ready for breakfast. He got dressed before me. In the interim, housekeeping showed up. We had all our valuables laid out in full view, so I'm trying to get ready and make sure that our things are in the safe.

I got downstairs, and he exploded. He was yelling and telling me that I was inconsiderate and disrespectful by having him wait for me so long. I tried to explain what had taken me so long, but he didn't hear any of that. That continued as we got on the little cart to go to the restaurant. While I was trying to explain, he took his empty water bottle and hit me in the head with it.

I yelled to the driver, "Stop this cart and let me off!" What has just happened? I called back to the States to my wedding coordinator, who also was my friend, and tell her what just popped off.

She was infuriated. "You mean to tell me, you are in Cancun, and this n.... has the nerve to hit you?"

I was frantic and crying, wondering, what do I do now? She was trying to calm me down. I was in Cancun on my honeymoon, and things were in a tizzy. I realized there was nothing that she can do. It did help, though, to tell someone. We smoothed the waters for the rest of the trip, but things were never the same.

We got back home and started opening the wedding cards, and he exploded again. I didn't understand what was going on at all. Had I entered the Twilight Zone? Had I been warped into an alternate dimension or universe? I looked at him as if I had married another one of Satan's imps. My baby daddy was the first relative. Were these two related? Things continued to unravel.

Scene II

I went into the bedroom and tried to resolve an argument that we had earlier. He yelled, in a rage, for me to get out of the room. His temper went from one to ten to twenty in a matter of seconds. I walked out of the room backward and fell to the ground. He was hovering over me, and Ki-Ki got involved. He pushed her out of the way to the floor, and this, for her, was her cue to call the police. She has been my rock and angel my entire life. The police arrived, and he was apologetic, of course. He explained how he had lost his temper, and he knew he should not have.

Scene III

On another occasion, I was at a function, and I got a call from Ki-Ki's father. He was ranting and screaming about Colby putting his hands on her. I called home to find out what was going on. I got the story from him, Ki-Ki, and my stepdaughter, Raynise. When it was all said and done, it was two against one. Ki-Ki and Raynise provided the same reenactment of the events. Ki-Ki called the police on him for the second time. The police advised him that he can't, under any circumstances, put his hands on her. The laws had changed so much that one couldn't hit one's own child, let alone someone else's. In my life, as it applied to me and mine, that law was non-applicable. I will never have to worry about my daughter. I have planted the, "No nonsense, no tolerance" seed in her. I don't know how, but I'm glad that I have.

Scene IV

On another occasion, Colby pushed me in a dispute. I lost it because what he ain't fixin' to do was get the idea that he's gonna put his hands on me, and there will be no repercussions. I'm the black chick from the hood. I raised my voice, and I pushed him back. The girls showed up, and he yelled and told them to go away. His daughter did, but not my Ki-Ki.

She didn't say anything but stood there as if to say, this is my momma, and I'm not going anywhere.

She approached me, "Ma, you good?"

She was looking at me like, you know I will make that call. (Hilarious)

I replied, "Yes, Baby, I'm good."

She never addressed him because it was all about her momma. His daughter had a real fear of him, but Ki-Ki had none.

There was argument after argument, and the time he put all my things on the lawn and told me to get the f(bleep) out! Our home never became a happy one. I was losing my mind. I would pray and cry, not wanting to go home. I found out later that he mistreated Ki-Ki. She told me he would buy food for Raynise, but not for her, and she would go hungry. I knew this from Ki-Ki's mouth, and his daughter told me, as well. That tore through my soul.

One time, Ki-Ki probed, "Why do you let him disrespect you as he does?"

"I have to be the woman of God that God called me to be, no matter what he says or does. God is looking at not how he treats me, but how I respond to his treatment.

"You are much better than I could be."

I knew that I had two girls looking at me as the woman. The message was not to be a punk but to be a Christian. I stood my ground, but I stayed saved.

The straw that broke the camel's back, and mine, happened one Sunday morning. Normally, I could let what he did and said kind of roll off my back, but this Sunday morning was different. Most arguments were on Sunday morning. Go figure. Old funky devil!

Scene V

It was Second Sunday, which was youth Sunday, and I was the youth choir director. I can't remember why we were arguing. He was yelling like a mad man. I went into another room and slammed the door. I had to remove myself from it as much as possible. He burst in like some crazed maniac, declaring that it was his house, and I didn't have the right to close the door. He spewed all kinds of obscenities at me. I was this, and I was that. I took it as long as I could. Tears were streaming down my face until I finally broke. I stood and got ready to speak, and God shut my mouth. Wayaminute. Why, God, why?

God told me," If you say what you want to say to Colby, it will break him, and he will never recover."

Yeah, and? That's the point!

God stated, "Your tongue is anointed. You will destroy him if you say what you want to say."

I didn't care. I knew I had enough. Colby thought I couldn't say anything to hurt him. Most people, who know me, know that's a fallacy. I would have not only cut Colby deeply and permanently with the words, but I would have shredded him into pieces like a meat grinder. What I wanted to say to him in retaliation for his cruelty was going to be a winner-winner, chicken dinner! I'm salivating now thinking about it. In the first chapter, I told you about the mind games that my father and I indulged in regularly. I always had a comeback. Always! I was the comeback queen. That goes to show you how ignorant Colby was. It was absurd to think that someone that lives with you sleeps with you, and knows you, wouldn't be able to say one thing that could cut deep.

I got angry with God. Yes, furious. He was still telling me how it was my responsibility to stand for righteousness. Words can't express how angry I was and how battered I felt. The girls and everyone at church saw it. I tried to hide it and disguise the pain. Not this time. -- I cried driving to church. The girls tried to console me, but nothing helped.

The tears are flowing now intensely as does blood from a punctured artery. I was trying to be strong for my girls but they are coming uncontrollably.

As I press through and attempt to regroup from what seems like a continuous heart spasm,

I must confess, if never again, right now, Broken I Am.

My next request was for God to release me. I walked past the mirror, and I had to do a double take because I didn't recognize myself. I was dying mentally, physically, and spiritually. I tried to get him to go to counseling, and he went, once. The counselor was bewildered because Colby controlled the entire session. The counselor and I couldn't get in a word edgewise. All he talked about was how he was married before, what a good husband he was, and how he knew how to have a good marriage. Unfortunately, his ex-wife was not there to affirm his claim. I needed to hear that confession from her for myself! Maybe by having a séance. Even his daughter had doubts, and she knew him better than anyone. Things are not always as they seem from the outside. No one can be that different, so great as a husband once and so horrible now. Nope! I don't believe it one bit. The Counselor and I had a session alone, and she asked me how I lived with him. She said they would've been divorced if she was his wife. She could tell he was very controlling, self-centered, and a narcissistic know it all. Yeah, but I loved-ed-ed him. If you ever love someone, you never stop. You just find purpose in knowing you are healthier apart than together.

The marriage was over, and I had to prepare to move. I had nowhere to go. I forgot to mention that the home I had originally spent all my hard-earned money on, went into foreclosure. That also crushed me. He refused to help me sell or rent it while we were together. Unbelievable. He was a real estate guru. Why would he allow income property to slip away? Because it was my house, he didn't see how it benefitted him in any way. He didn't help me because I didn't matter, so he expended neither time nor effort to devote any attention to it or how I felt regarding it. **JERK!**

As I was trying to move and come up with the money for the things my daughter and I needed, there were times that I'd ask him to help. He offered me deals. He said for everything thing that I purchased for the house, and that was remaining, he would give me half the value. What an ass! Forgive me, but that is how I felt at the time. I had sold everything, moved into his house, and gave him the money for the things I sold. I was in a position where I had to cow down. I had nothing. I had no furniture except a chaise and some paintings. I asked him if he would buy me a bedroom set, and he told me he had to think about it. He didn't. I don't know what a heart attack feels like, but I know that there are symptoms of an aching that resonates in your arm and your jaw. Well, however that feels, paralleled what I felt with my broken heart and what I ardently expressed as, Pain.

Scene VI

I moved on my birthday, Dec. 2, 2006. What a birthday gift. The movers were there, and the cost exceeded what I had. I ask Colby to help me, and he told me he didn't have his wallet on him. He could've gone to the bank or left to get his wallet. I was bawling as I called my baby brother. He rescued me, as always.

Sidebar: *If there is a real man in your life, ask him questions about men. Only a man knows how a man thinks. My brother despised him, and only now do I see why. He tried to tell me, but who listens to their brother?*

I moved with nothing, but God gave me a house (with no money down, a bankruptcy, and a foreclosure on my credit) for us to live in fully furnished.

My daughter needed a bedroom set. I walked into the neighborhood furniture store and applied for credit. It was declined, of course.

The man told me, "You look familiar."

I replied, "I have purchased furniture here before, some years back. I just moved back to Indiana, and my daughter needs a bedroom set."

"I tell you what I'll do. If you promise to give me "x" amount of money a month, I'll give you the bedroom set."

Who does that? Or, my favorite saying, where they do that at? God supplied all that I needed with no money and so-so credit, even my bedroom set from Value City. I walked in, picked it out, and they denied my credit.

I stole away to a corner. "God, this is what I want, and I need you to make it happen for me."

Even though they denied me credit the first time, I still walked out with it that day. He supplied furniture in every room where we needed it. Even after yet another failure and disappointment, why God loves me so much, I will never know. But I'm thankful. God has been so good to me! Praise your name, God.

I experienced mixed feelings about the move. Ki-Ki was elated. I grieved because I was leaving my other daughter and my marriage behind. We are all wishing she could come with us. I'm on my own and still not free from the "soul tie." I held on, but not to God's unchanging hand.

People that have never experienced divorce can't relate to the devastation of it. It feels like death, but in a way, far worse. At least in death, you have no choice but to deal with it and come to realize that no matter what, you can't recapture or resuscitate that lost love. What do you do when the person is still living and has your heart? I wanted to stay, but I knew I had to leave. I wanted so desperately to walk backward, but I had to run forward. I went through this excess of conflicting emotions that made me feel like a tsunami would save me from my misery. Any cataclysmic occurrence would serve me better than being a participant in this perpetual cycle of torture and grief. Not to mention, all the lonely nights I knew were ahead. I have my daughter, but she holds a different place in my heart. The place that he held felt like someone had it in their hand and wrung it like a wet towel. With all the progressive technology and scientific discoveries, they can make a condom to protect genitalia from infectious sexual diseases, but no one has yet made a condom to protect the heart from the effectual crushing blows of lost love.

During all of this, I was watching Oprah one day. She became the impetus to my "Ah-Ha" moment and awakened something in me that I had suppressed. I hadn't realized that I had been molested. In hindsight, I see how my life was deeply impacted by it. It left an imprint in every relationship that I had up until that point and even beyond the recollection. I had suppressed all thoughts about it, and all the memories had been tucked away in the crevices of my mind and lost like an artifact from the Ice Age. I'm glad that it was uncovered, but only God could bring clarity and understanding to that rare find. This was not like an archaeological find of any other kind.

Every emotion that I felt replayed in my mind as if I was watching it on video. All the anguish I felt when it happened, I felt then. All the horrible thoughts I had when it happened, I thought then. Tears, tears, and more tears. What effect has this had on my behavior and my decisions? I tried to make sense of my entire life. The person that I was, I didn't even know. I needed to relearn who I was.

I immediately called my niece, Victoria, to tell her of my revelation. Next, I told my brother Christopher, and then my mother. As I began to share my experience, others in my family did, as well. My mother started to take it personally. She felt that she hadn't done all she could to protect me because her stepfather had molested her when she was a child. I had to reassure her that it wasn't her fault. How could she possibly know? She entrusted me into the care of my older brother. It wasn't his fault, either. This occurrence was a part of my destiny and my purpose. I didn't call him and tell him because I didn't want him to feel like he was culpable, as if he was negligible in watching his baby sister. I wanted to save him from the truth. It was what it was.

Whether we like it or not, our experiences shape who we are. Our way of thinking, our reasoning, and psyche all stem from occurrences and events from our past. The molestation had set a precedent for my behavior with men, but I had not realized it yet. Why did I hang on to men so long? Why was I accepting of anything, no matter how ridiculous? Why, why, why? There were so many unanswered questions, Lord. Maybe with this revelation, some healing could begin. I don't know for sure, but at least it was a start.

That awakening was the beginning of my road to healing. I was grateful but wounded. A lot of people find it hard to understand how someone can suppress something for so long. The brain is such a complex mechanism. Anyone can bury anything in the mind if it's painful enough, yet the mind is capable of total recall, given the right stimuli.

I had an opportunity to confront Todd about what happened.

I informed him, "You know you molested me, right?"

He responded, "We never had sex," and then chuckled as if to controvert what I said.

"We did everything else, and I was twelve!"

"Well. if you feel that I molested you, then I apologize."

If I feel that he molested me? Wow!

Todd had worked in the school system for years, and I pray that he didn't molest anyone else. I don't believe that I was the special chosen one, though. Most that do this to one have also done it to another. I pray now that if he did, God would reach into that shattered place of damage and despair and heal whoever she is, in the name of Jesus. Amen.

I forgave him. He is the one that must reconcile with his Father, not me. I knew that I must forgive him for my recovery. I realized that I had a long way to go. I had uncovered the source, but not all the areas of restoration. There were so many layers to be exposed, and issues addressed. I still didn't see the connection fully. The strings were still loose.

8

The Emancipation: Got Free but Can't Get Right

I will look back on this and realize it

helped me secure my fate.

This too shall pass, and going forward

I will never forget Jan. 5, 2008.

For this was the day that God released me

from the baggage, this was my Independence Day!

Colby and I continued to have a sexual relationship. We were still married, and we had needs. That was a dangerous place. Sex creates connections, and this kept me connected. Colby and I were talking everything through to make sense of it all. None of it ever did make sense. How about this as an answer: We were not meant to be! I missed the companionship, especially the warm body next to me at night. Humans, with our infinite complexities, always want to make something out of nothing.

I toggled back and forth with Colby, but then I meet Elder Alowishus Washington. I didn't plan on getting involved with him. He wasn't my type either. (What is with these men that are not my type?) I'm a fitness guru, and he was larger than I preferred. I convinced myself that I needed a friend. The friend I needed was Jesus. There's not a friend like the lowly Jesus. No not one, no, not one." I realized that, later.

Alowishus hung around all the time, and things became comfortable. He pined vigorously for my attention. I kept telling him I was still in love with Colby. The fact that he couldn't have me made him try even harder. The more I pulled away, the closer he pushed. I looked at Alowishus and thought, maybe, even after many told me that I was treading in dangerous waters.

They were screaming, "Put on your life jacket and swim to shore!"

I decided that everyone had a past, and we all deserved a second chance. Here she comes, "Super Karen." Hold on a minute and let me grab my cape. We all do deserve a second chance, but that should be granted by God and God alone. At least in this instance.

Sidebar: *Ladies, we are not heroes or saviors. We need to stop trying to save these men. Let God save them, and then let God lead. Take the capes off! You are not and will never be a superhero. You cannot change or save anyone from anything, especially when they don't want to change or be saved! One of my favorite lines from "Jason's Lyric," "You can't save a brother that don't wanna be saved." You can't even save yourself!*

I decided to file for divorce after already "kind-a sort-a" starting something with Alowishus. I went to City Hall to get the appropriate papers needed to file for divorce. I asked for the necessary papers.

The clerk said to me, "But there's no record of a marriage."

"What, no, record?! Check again."

She did, and the conclusion was the same.

She affirmed, "There is no record of a marriage!" There was only a request for the marriage license.

"So, you are telling me that I'm not legally married?"

She explained that if we had a ceremony, we were, but there are no papers filed in the system to prove it. To me, that meant that not only has God freed me from the marriage, but he made it non-existent in the system. "Be us free!" (Remember the movie, Amistad?) If this is not a sign and a wonder, then I don't know what is. All I had to do was walk away. Karen, walk away. Fade off into the distance. Nope, not me!

I was free on paper, but my heart wouldn't let go. Why was I still thinking that there was a maybe? Our relationship was deeply rooted, like a one-hundred-year-old oak tree. Like a tornado can uproot one of those trees, God can uproot and break that "soul tie." It's a choice.

We still saw each other, and then the unimaginable happened to me. I had been with him about two days before, and I showed up at his house per usual. I knocked and knocked. I knew he was there, but he never answered the door or the phone. It was obvious. He was in there with another woman. I had all I could take. God showed me that to liberate me. It was my Independence Day!

9

The Evolution: Starting to Progress

Yet again I think why me, why can't I find a place of

solitude during this storm,

Someplace that will shield me, cover me,

keep me safe and warm?

Well yet again, I must start over and, through God, rebuild

all that has been lost,

I entered this without adding up the cost.

Yet again, here I am...damn, damn, damn.

When we think of the Israelites, we think of God delivering them out of bondage. No matter what signs God showed them, many still didn't believe. Moses' staff turned the Nile to blood, and the waters parted as they crossed the Red Sea. What else did they need to see? They were no different from us today. God shows us things as clear as day, and we are caught back in Egypt and enslaved by our wants and desires. One is sure to be bound and remain bound if you take your eyes off the Lord. Welcome to my Egypt.

I tried to get over Colby and move into this, whatever it was, with Alowishus. My brother had a conversation with me about him. He told me all the things that he had done and the relationships he had been in, but I didn't listen. I'm so bull-headed. Who listens to their brother?

I asked Ki-Ki what she thought about it. She discerned the men in my life well. She warned me about a few things, but who listens to their daughter? She told me that she didn't have anything against him, personally, and it wasn't that she didn't like him. She didn't like him for me. She mentioned that it wasn't anything she could pinpoint per se.' It was just something that didn't sit well with her.

Sidebar: *I have asked, "Who listens to their mother, brother, and daughter?" facetiously several times. The truth of the matter is if you are going to surround yourself with* *people that you trust, you need to listen, at least, sometimes. God can and will send a word through other people. The best recourse, of course, is to seek God, but there are those that He uses with insight that will tell you the truth. Shut up, sat down, and LISTEN! After all, God can use an ass to deliver a message. I'm just saying. Don't be so quick to beat the messenger.*

I ran from Alowishus emotionally for a long time. He was close, but not too close, and then it happened. I let my defenses down. I was in a vulnerable state and was like a piece of driftwood on the ocean, moving, tossed, and lost emotionally and spiritually.

I was no longer happy at the church I attended. Not because they had done anything wrong, I was simply craving more of a spiritual connection. I had been in a dry place for a while, maybe about a year, but it was coming to a head. I had been in ministry since 2003, and it was 2008. My life started to do another nosedive. This time was the worst ever. Why couldn't I stay focused? There was always some man that I let in that took me off the beaten path.

My mother pleaded with me over and over, "Stay focused; stay focused!" Who listens...? This new relationship almost killed me.

After I received information about him, I had a candid conversation about it with him. I explained that if he desired to be anything to me, there needed to be full disclosure. If I catch you in a lie, it's over. There was nothing worse. We covered all of what I thought necessary to move forward. I had told him from the beginning that I wasn't ready to get into anything, but he kept hanging around. He was married three times, so he said, and recently divorced, and I was coming out of one.

Three months in, Bertha, his ex-wife, knocked at the door. I was shocked! She stood at my door and asked if she could come in and talk to me. I opened the door and scanned my kitchen for weapons. People are crazy, and she had come to my domain. I was at ease, but on guard. She told me he was a liar. He had been telling her that he wanted to reconcile. She mentioned how he has been married four times, not three, and how they had spent the night together a few days ago. That sparked a memory:

Alowishus was a security guard. There was one night when he told me he was going to stop by. Now I knew that he didn't get off until ten o'clock, which would have put him at my house by ten-thirty. Close to the time that he was supposed to arrive, I called him. No answer. That wasn't like him. I got a little worried. I called a couple more times to no avail and went to sleep.

He stopped by the next day.

My first question was, "What happened? I thought you were coming by last night."

"Yeah, the guy I was working with needed a ride home, so I took him"

"Okay.... you couldn't call me and tell me that?"

"My phone ran out of power, and I didn't have my charger."

"The man you took home didn't have a phone?"

"No, he is Mexican. You know Mexican people don't have cellphones."

"What? Mexican people don't have cellphones? Are you kidding me?"

"I mean, he didn't have a cellphone."

"So, you are telling me that no one around that whole place had a phone that you could use. What about inside the restaurant?"

"By the time all this occurred, the restaurant was closed."

Bertha also told me that they spent the night together at a hotel.

I inquired," What night was this?"

I was accessing my memory bank. It was the same night that supposedly Raul, had no cellphone. I have put two and two together. One thing about math it's an absolute science. However, I was not invested in this relationship, yet. *(Sprint Karen, Run, Do a mad dash Karen!)* I told her I didn't know what they had going on, but he and I were just friends, and she could have him. I told her that he was on his way to my house, and she was more than welcome to confront him. I was calling, and she was texting. I wondered what was going on. She had spent three hours in my living room, filling me in on all that drama. Lord, what in the world is this mess? I must be crazier than a Betsy bug even to be entertaining this. I'm too old for this foolishness.

Alowishus had told me that she was nothing to him. That he wanted a new start, and he wanted it with me. Blah, blah, blah. That should have been my exit cue, but I allowed myself to take on a permanent role in this made for tv, "*Lifetime movie.*"

He did not show up, and it was probably purposed that he had not. As mentioned before. Romans 8:28

Sidebar: *If a woman is bold enough to show up at your door, at your door, at your door, there is a reason, and one should take heed. I don't care what is going on, I'm not going to another woman's house. I am not calling her trying to figure out, decipher, or "CSItize (homemade word) anything. It has not been, and never will be, that serious. There are usually red flags. We just tend to ignore them. Normally our Instincts are correct. This was probably red flag number 5, but I have on my "shero" cape. Cuz I in all* *my mighty powers can fix it! Hollering, "She's a bird, she's a plane... She's "Super Karen" NOT!*

Act VI - Scene I

Alowishus arrived 30 minutes after Bertha left. I asked where he was. He told me some long, elaborate story. He always had one. He could make up a story on a dime. As smart as he was, paralleled how dumb he was. His grasp of the English language and vernacular was bar none, but he was defunct of common sense. He was eloquent and charismatic when he spoke.

Bertha had armed me with all this ammunition, so I interrogated him.

"Guess who just left here?"

He fidgeted, "Who?"

"Bertha.."

"Bertha, why was she here?"

I laughed. "She was giving me some information."

"Information like what?"

I was still laughing. "Well, how many times have you been married?"

He shifted nervously.

"Never mind. She told me that you were married four times, and you told me three."

"The first time it was only for some months, and it was annulled."

"You can't get an annulment unless there is a marriage, dummy. You really are stupid."

He had a stupid look on his face.

"Guess what else she said?"

He glanced at me.

"Remember the night you told me that "Mexicans don't have cellphones" story - explaining why you didn't call me or come by?"

"Yes."

"Bertha told me you were at the hotel with her." I chuckled.

He stuttered, "I, I, I, I, I, I... This is what happened. I called her up to talk to her. I felt like I needed a clean slate, so I wanted to apologize to her. I wanted her to know that if I caused her any pain, I was sorry. I didn't want to move into something without a clear conscience."

"This is the woman that you claim is crazy, a stalker, will not leave you alone, and keeps calling you.

You have a guilty conscience about what again? Which lie is the truth? And what about the hotel thing?"

"She came to the restaurant where I was."

"How did she know that was where you were working? You know what?"

"I told her to meet me there."

"You had the crazy, stalker woman meet you at the place where you work? You did this why, again? I'm

just trying to understand why this couldn't have been accomplished by phone."

"I thought that she deserved for me to apologize in person."

I shook my head, "You are dumber than I thought. I'm still trying to understand the hotel."

I got in her car....

I interrupted, "Wait, you got in the car with the crazy stalker?"

"She started driving and wouldn't let me out. She told me that we were going to the hotel, and she wasn't letting me out of the car."

"I'm still stuck on the fact that you got in the car with the crazy stalker. Now, okay, you are at the hotel. After you arrived there, you didn't think to yourself to call me to come and get you?"

"I knew you would be angry after I told you where I was and..."

I pushed him in the forehead. That was the least I could do. I don't advise it, but it was that or curse him out.

"You think me finding out this way would make me happy? You know what? I'm not angry. I'm just grateful for the information."

He cried and apologized.

"Quit crying."

"I know I have betrayed your trust, but I promise you nothing happened. I will make it up to you. Please give me another chance."

My dumb ass, I mean self, did just that.

Sidebar: *Don't fall for the Okie Doke. Crying, really? I've been around quite a few men, from friends, family, associates, etc.... and I have never known one to break out crying over something like this. We are three months in. Really, Dude? Really? It's a part of the scam. Those who cry on a whim, this is a part of what they do. Trust and believe! On My Momma!*

We continued dating for about six to eight months. I was still trying to fight off falling for him, but I'm falling into the trap. He became a filler. Someone to fill the void of loneliness, but it was causing me more harm than good. He was around all the time, driving my car, washing his clothes at my house; we had a joint cellphone bill, etc. He was daily professing his undying love for me. He wanted to get married. I was getting cards and handwritten letters of confessions and expressions. I had, by then, succumbed to *it*. Whatever *it* was.

Sidebar: *He was just in love with the idea of love and not a clue as to what it means to be loved and married. Marriage and love are not what you say, but what you do. Four times before? Look, don't think that you are special. I have since found out that he married, again twice, divorced, and remarried. Seriously?! I told him perhaps he should consider being like Paul, single. Well, seven is the number of completion. So, maybe it could've been me as an ex-wife. Lord! Thank you!*

A year into our relationship, he started acting strange. I saw a number on the phone bill a lot. I, of course, confronted him about it, but he said she was just a friend. While on the phone with my niece, Vicky, I mentioned the young lady to her, and she mentioned that she knew her. They were sorority sisters. She told me that the girl was posting on Facebook about some minister that she was dating. The young lady had mentioned something about being a "First Lady." Vicky said she believed the young lady had been in my car. I ignored this because I was all in. Well, maybe not ignored, but it wasn't sinking in. This couldn't be happening. He had pursued me for almost a year. He loves me; he loves me! Or so I thought. I did need therapy.

Scene II

He was at my house, taking a nap. My intuition kicked in and told me to look at his phone. Now, this is something I never did, but I picked it up, and I saw endearing text messages and then, the nail in the coffin, naked pictures.

I confronted him about it, and the entire thing flipped on me. "This is your fault," he accused. "I was tired of waiting for you."

I probed, "Huh. What? Waiting for me to do what? You are at my house every day, eating my food, and driving my car."

We had been dating for almost a year now? We were attached at the hip and did everything together. Well, not everything because he was slipping and dipping.

An intense sensation came over me. I felt like someone kicked me in the gut with their foot. My head spun like I was in a tornado. I couldn't catch my breath. There were tears, nervousness, and anxiety. I was losing my mind. What in the heck was happening here? I was shaking, dizzy, and I felt like I needed to throw up! I felt things toward him that I had never felt before.

I had been married and divorced twice, but this was like a demonic attack. My chest felt like it was caving in, and I was hyperventilating. Feelings of fear, agony, and hopelessness came over me. I couldn't deal with the rejection. I yielded to a man who wasn't even my type. I took him in and nurtured him. Built him up and helped him lose weight. Polished him like brass, and then this! I screamed inside. I had a dam "soul tie" with him. People don't believe that spirits can transfer. Spirits are real, and they can and will transfer if you are not spiritually guarded. I had no Holy Ghost; therefore, I had no power and nothing to ward off this attack. I know the only reason that this didn't take me out was that my mother was constantly praying for me. Thanks, mom.

End Scene

When we first met, he was deeply depressed. I never really thought that if I connected with him, there would be a possibility of that spirit attaching itself to me. But before I knew it, it had. I was more depressed than ever. It was the worst condition I had ever experienced. I begged him to stay with me. It was me, Karen Dade, begging for Alowishus to stay with me?! Crazy, for real. I wish the hell I would, ever again, but this was who I was.

I cried all the time and lost weight. I was already small and couldn't afford to lose weight? The enemy had set a trap for me, and since I wasn't spiritually connected, I didn't see it and fell deep into it. He had stolen my joy and killed my spirit, so the only thing left was to literally kill me.

My mother implored, "Karen, you have to shake this off."

I replied, "I'm trying."

I was waking up in the middle of the night, calling out to God and crying copiously. I was tormented every day, all day. I cried myself to sleep every night. It was so bad that I crying myself to wake. Sounds strange but if you have ever been there, you understand. My angel, Kianna, consoled me on several occasions. She was so encouraging, trying to rebuild me in my brokenness. She kept telling me that I was a good person, beautiful and that he was undeserving of me. She told me I was going to make it; trust God. Just trust God! I was so far from what she expressed to me. I had lost myself. I couldn't hear her. The enemy was trying desperately to kill me, everything about me, everything that was in me, and everything that was purposed for me. I was so bound by this spirit.

According to my niece, I had called her all the time, asking her to pray for me. I had no recollection of those calls or the prayers I requested. She said I told her that I was unable to pray. The enemy had me in such a place that I couldn't pray or even hear her pray. I'm just grateful that something in me made me call her because without someone covering and interceding for me, I would've been lost. That is why you should surround yourself with godly people. There just might come a time that you can't pray. You can be in something so deep and be so far removed from God that the prayers of others are all you have. Thank God the prayers of the righteous availeth much!

Scene III

One night, my wailing woke Kianna. She asked what was wrong. I couldn't talk or breathe. I felt like my lungs were collapsing, and I was having an aneurysm. The pain in my chest was excruciating. I was having an anxiety attack. I had Ki-Ki call my mom. I didn't know what to do. She called 911. The ambulance came and checked my vitals. I was fine, thank God. I was fine physically, but in every other way, I wasn't.

The paramedic asked me, "Was there a recent break-up or something?"

All I could do was nod and hang my head. Why didn't I listen to all those around me when they told me to run as fast as I could? No, not me; so, through all my obstinacy, I find myself here... Yet Again.

The last straw was when I got a message on Facebook from "The Other Woman." She told me personal things about myself, and she called me "Eviligist." (a nice play on "Evangelist." I had to give it to her). By this time, I was getting over it. I called her, we talked, and I told her I was out, and she could have him. I disconnected from God, but he had not removed the hedge of protection. He still had me covered by His blood. If he had not, I know, without a doubt, I would have been dead.

I started visiting New Zion Temple in August of 2009. I gave my letter of resignation to New Hope Missionary Baptist Church in September. I was searching, yearning, needing something, and needing it fast.

I was visiting and visiting the church until one day, my daughter looked at me, "Mom, don't you think it's time?" It was time. We joined on Oct. 18, 2009. That was the beginning of my evolution. I knew that was where God had sent me. I would never have chosen that place, but that place chose me. It was all good because it was all God! It truly was the Lord's doing.

10

The Enlightenment: The Darkness Uncovered

I need you right now and, in this place,

Please fill the void in this huge and lonely, empty space.

I know that only you love me unconditionally and cherish me for the gift that I am,

This, too, shall pass, and all that the enemy meant to steal, kill, and destroy, you will restore, renew, and amend.

I needed to get refocused. I'm a minister. God sent me to a place that can get me back to him and back into the place I needed to be for the next phase of my life. There were still some dark places because I had recently moved out of Egypt, a place of bondage. I knew that moving to this place was what God meant for me because there are so many places left for Him to repair.

October 2009. I was a member of the New Zion Temple Church. This was the best thing that could've happened to me from a holistic perspective. I needed something that would speak to my dark places. Every branch of this tree that held all my issues needed pruning. So, Lord, Let the pruning begin!

One Sunday morning, my pastor, Bishop Brandon A. Jacobs, Sr., preached an unforgettable sermon about snakes. He has such an anointing on his life. God had empowered him with what I needed to start breaking the chains of bondage, destroying the yokes that so heavily weighed me down and to mend the broken places of my life.

I remember Ki-Ki looked at me and dittoed the things he mentioned. He talked about how you must be careful not to be in the company of snakes. He explained how a boa constrictor would coil itself around its prey until it squeezes the life out of it. He does not want his prey dead. It wants to experience the pleasure of sucking the life out of it; bone by bone, and vertebrae by vertebrae until the heart stops. It's the same concept as snaky people. They will stay around you pretending to be your friend and on your side. All the while, they are sucking up all the air around you. You wonder why you feel like you have COPD (chronic obstructive pulmonary disease). You can't freely breathe when they are around. Instead of them building you up, they are secretly hating on you and squeezing the life out of you. They are poison. They get closer as you weaken until they kill your spirit, steal your purpose, and destroy your destiny.

That was the day I had a breakthrough. The pastor told us to go home and anoint everything in the house; every wall, window, doorknob, and anything else that might be carrying a spirit of oppression and depression. He said to include the people in the house. I couldn't get home fast enough.

The enemy is cunning. Church ended, and while I was walking to my car, I got this long text from Alowishus:

I'm sorry for causing you pain. I didn't intend for things to happen the way they did, but I am in love with her and want to spend the rest of my life with her. "

That son of a b(bleep). I wasn't the only one that would benefit from counseling. How was avidly professing his love for me not more than a month ago and now her? Never mind! I read his text and was emotionless. Many things ran through my head.

I read it to my daughter, and she shook her head and said, "That's the devil."

I concurred.

I had just received my release from that foolishness and then this. I sat there, thinking about how I should respond. I asked Ki-Ki.

"Mom, is it really worth it?"

From the mouths of babes!

I agreed, "No."

I never responded and pressed forward with my life.

That chapter of my life was finally over. It drained me to degrees that I can't explain. The devil had a plan for me, one that he devised in his conspiracy to take me out. One thing that I can say assuredly, though, I'm plain Tired.

My heart is telling me, "You will heal, and you will feel again."

To not have faith is very much a tragic sin.

Knowing this, I will press on; towards the mark, I will aspire.

But man, when I think about it all, mentally and emotionally, I'm plain Tired.

I was on the road back to my first love, Jesus Christ. I was getting prophecy after prophecy about a women's ministry. I knew it, but to what degree, I had no idea. I had been teaching and speaking about it but couldn't see the big picture. There must be a total recovery to proceed in the way that God can use you the most. How can one minister on healing, if they have never been sick, and then healed? Where I was, is where God had been trying to get me - Healed and Acquitted from the scars of my past.

Sex was still an issue, but I thought I had it under control. I had an issue with masturbation. I didn't see how it could be wrong. I wasn't hurting anyone. There is nothing in the Bible that talks about this except that one scripture (Genesis 38:9), and I'm not spilling my seed on the ground. That scripture has nothing to do with masturbation.

It's astounding how we can find all types of rationales to do wrong but can't find the same to do right. We can convince ourselves of anything and try to justify it. However, the closer you get to God, the more he reveals himself to you; and the more he reveals yourself to you. You can run, but you shole' can't hide.

11

The Exhortation: My Appeal

Tears are now streaming down the sides of each one of my cheeks,

I'm not concerned about who may walk by or who might be privy to see.

If I'm asked, I will just simply tell them that, "All that I am, and all that I could ever hope to be,"

Oh God, my Lord, and my King, I owe it all unto none other than Unto Thee!

I was under much Holy Ghost power and anointing Sunday after Sunday, but I was still beating myself up repeatedly because of my past. I felt so unworthy of my life calling. God, why did you choose me? I had never told my older brother about the molestation, but I realized that that was a part of my healing. I had to tell him, so I did.

I called him and told him what happened. I had to preface the conversation by saying that it wasn't his fault, and I didn't blame him. I didn't want him to feel responsible in any way. It wasn't about him, my parents, or even the predator. It was about me. That freed me some, but not totally. There were still some branches on the tree that hadn't been pruned yet, and some roots not dug up.

I was on the phone with First Lady Anita Roberts of New Hope in Gary one day. We were talking, and I was sharing. While this was happening, and she was ministering to me, God revealed that I had a problem with rejection. The issue with men was why I had rejected God; not understanding that there was a parallel. I was unconsciously rejecting him. We cried and praised. That night was such an awakening for me. It was another step toward healing.

I prayed, "God, please let the real healing begin."

I realized that the reason I couldn't receive God's love (Him being a man), was because I couldn't deal with the possibility of Jesus (a man) rejecting me. I thought of him on the same level as a mortal man. I condemned myself all the time. Every time I thought about my sin, I was grieving. Nevertheless, Hallelujah, God is greater than our condemnation.

"For if our heart condemns us, God is greater than our heart and knows all things." I John 3:20 KJV

"For God sent not his Son into the world to condemn the world; but that the world through him might be saved. He that believeth on him is not condemned: but he that believeth not is condemned already because he hath not believed in the name of the only begotten Son of God." John 3:17 - 18 KJV

All of this stemmed from my first experience with rejection at the age of twelve. Wow! That was why I couldn't let go, even when letting go was the best choice. We continued to cry, praise, and worship on the phone for a while. It was refreshing and liberating to understand my behavior. I'm grateful that God allowed this conversation to take place, and I'm glad that Lady Anita was open to the Holy Spirit in her ministering to me. I was still in the beginning phases of my exordium but thank God for this step.

I had convinced myself that masturbation was not a sin because of a conversation I had previously with a pastor that I respected. He told me that it wasn't a conclusive issue, so when I needed to use it for myself, I could. I indulged in this behavior at least once a week. I needed a release because my body had urges. I couldn't have sex, so this was the next best thing. It was fulfilling at first. Then something happened. It was fulfilling one time, and not fulfilling the next time. Have you ever eaten a meal that satisfied the hunger pangs, but not the taste buds? After you finished it, you thought to yourself, "Man, I should have eaten something else, I could've had a V-8. You ate it because you didn't want to be hungry, but if you had another option, you would have chosen differently. Well, that is how it started to feel to me. It wasn't emotionally satisfying either. There is nothing like the real thing, the warmth, and intimacy between a man and a woman. Although, for some, it may suffice. I was doing it, but it wasn't gratifying. I wondered why I was doing it. The more I did it, the more dissatisfying it became. Sometimes, it was painful afterward. I believe that it was psychosomatic. It had become unsatisfying to my body and my mind, even though it was climatic. My body urged and surged so much, though. That sex demon wouldn't let me rest. The Holy Ghost was making it a place that was uncomfortable and unsatisfying, but I needed more than that to end it, and the Lord knew it. A couple of times, I even watched some porn. Now that was ridiculous. The good thing was that the Holy Ghost kicked in and wouldn't allow that door to open. Haven't you had enough? You are tripping. That ended quickly. What most don't understand is that when sin is in you, and you fix it one way, it will attempt to creep up in another way until it's healed.

For example, I have this bush in my front yard that I have cut down to the ground several times. To passersby, the bush appears to be dead, and it appears that way to me as well. Every spring, there is a branch that starts to sprout up from it, and it grows all over again. The roots are in the soil and continue to grow. The only way to kill it is with pesticide, or to dig it up from the root. Sin is no different.

I had confronted the molestation, the rejection, the sex, and then I had to see masturbation for what it was, sin! Sin never wants to go, so it will plant itself and stay rooted if it can. It will sprout and re-sprout. It takes a true desire for change, and then you must be open to hear and yield to the Holy Spirit.

I was on the phone one day with Bishop Dontrell Charles. He was one of my spiritual mentors. We were engaged in this revelatory conversation. Thank God for Bishop D. He is my big baby brother in the ministry. God will surround you with people that can help you get to the next place and get you free. I always ask God to show me, me, and on this day, He did. When you know better, you yield better.

I mentioned to him that I struggled with masturbation. He listened calmly, as he always did, while I babbled on with all my justifications for my behavior.

He inquired, "Are you done?"

Sometimes I can't stand him. (Just kidding) He is a straight shooter, and I love that about him.

I respond, "Yes."

He starts ministering to my spirit. He gives me the scripture:

"The acts of the flesh are obvious: sexual immorality, impurity, and debauchery; idolatry and witchcraft; hatred, discord, jealousy, fits of rage, selfish ambition, dissensions, factions 21 and envy; drunkenness, orgies, and the like. I warn you, as I did before, that those who live like this will not inherit the kingdom of God." Galatians 5:19 NIV

Several scriptures deal with lust. There is also scripture about your body being a temple of the Holy Spirit. The root of it all is lust. If you have ever masturbated, can you do it without lustful thoughts? There is always a visual picture of something in your mind. Is this not what drives the act? The whole act is sexual, with the end being an orgasm. Again, you can find a reason to justify anything, but if this walk or journey, to be a Christian is one of holiness, and it is, then all things must be pure. To be even blunter about it, do you believe for a moment that Our Lord and Savior was a masturbator? Enough said!

There are and will be several people who will read the scriptures and turn them into something other than what they are. I'm not here to convince anyone of anything. I have given you the word. You can read the Scriptures for yourself and let God reveal himself to you. For me, instantly, there was a conviction. I didn't have to go to counseling or attend a "twelve-step" program, though I know that for some people, in certain instances, these programs are extremely helpful. (If you have a made-up mind, you can be healed instantly just like the woman with the issue of blood) Mark 5:25-29.

I was finally at the place where I wanted to be free from all the things that would be a hindrance and displeasing to God. I was able to receive and, in the place that I needed to be in to get delivered from myself. Hallelujah! If this is your desire, then the yolk of bondage that is on you can be destroyed as well.

You can't ask God to show you, if you are not ready to see it, accept it, and surrender it to Him. He showed me, I accepted it, I repented and never did it again, for an exceptionally long time. I'm transparent. The thoughts still cross my mind, and the urges are prevalent in my flesh. *"Whom the Son sets free is free indeed." John 8:36 KJV*

It's one day at a time. However, I can proclaim that now I'm Free! I must die daily, like Paul. I'm winning more than I'm losing. Praise God, and I'm no longer bound. I know how to combat the urge with the word and the Holy Ghost that rests, rules, and abides within me. *"Flee from sexual immorality. All other sins a person commits are outside the body, but whoever sins sexually, sins against their own body." I Corinthians 6:19.* I realize that my body is a temple of the Holy Ghost, and I take pride in this fact. My body is not my own, and I want it used by God. I want the anointing, and I want His glory. That place of freedom was a place that I not only needed to stay in, but I wanted to stay. It was a choice. I chose God, and I chose holiness!

Finally, I was on the right track. God was daily confirming who I was in Him but I was oblivious to it all. It's mind-blowing how gracious He has been to me. I firmly confess that I owe my life, God, To Thee.

12

The Election: Oh, To Be Chosen

"I Never Knew"

I never knew someone would love me so deeply,

To look beyond all my faults and love me completely. I never knew I could have a love to call my own,

That would bring me such peace and I'd never again be alone.

I never knew I could have joy inside of tears,

That would ease the pain and relieve all my doubts and all my fears. Lord, you made the difference.

The path and the journey that led me to the place where I am now wasn't one that I would've chosen for myself. God reminds me often of this scripture, and it continually resonates in my mind and my spirit:

"Before I formed you in the womb, I knew you, before you were born, I set you apart; I appointed you as a prophet to the nations." Jeremiah 1:5 NIV. He knew me before the foundations of the world, and yet, He chose me!

"Moreover, whom he did predestinate, them he also called: and whom he called, them he also justified: and whom he justified, them he also glorified." Romans 8:30 KJV

I had nothing to do with this. He Chose Me, and I praise Him for it!

While writing this book, God allowed me to minister twice on molestation. Two people came forth and admitted they shared similar experiences. One said to me that he wouldn't change a thing. When I was told this, at first, I didn't share that same sentiment. I told him that if I could, I would.

Then I entered a conversation with my baby brother about it. I shared with him my feelings on the subject. We talked for a while about, if I could go back to change my life, knowing, of course, what I know now, would I change it?

He proposed some things to me.

He clearly stated, "Think about it. If you did change your life, who would you be? Would you be the person you are today? Not only that, in changing things, you would alter all the other things in your life, including the people. All the events and outcomes would be different."

It reminded me of the movie, The Butterfly Effect."." It was a movie where the main character was able to read from his diary, think about it intensely, and go back and change it. He did this a few times. Once, he ended up in jail. Another time, the girl that he loved so much was a junky/prostitute, and another time he had paraplegia.

After our conversation, I was grateful for who I was. Your fate is your fate. Your purpose is your purpose. Your destiny is your destiny.

My brother continued, "God knew that you would be able to handle it, and he chose you to carry the load that brought you to where you are right now."

Like God sent his Son to be the sacrificial lamb for the atonement of our sins, some are chosen to operate in the same capacity. We were chosen as a sacrifice to go thru and tell others of His goodness despite our circumstances. I can say now that I am grateful that I made it. God brought me through so that I can minister to the pain and hurt of another victim, to encourage them to press on, because freedom is on the other side of the press. Hallelujah!

The second person was a female who reminded me of myself. She was steadily looking for love in all the wrong places. She was in such a dark place. I understood it. I had been there. She told me that it was as if God wasn't hearing her, and she couldn't hear Him.

I probed, "Who moved?"

We must ask ourselves, are we close enough to Him for Him to hear us, and close enough to Him to hear Him? You can't have a relationship with someone that you don't spend time with or communicate.

I told her, "You must return to your first love."

"Nevertheless, I have somewhat against thee, because thou hast left thy first love. Remember therefore from whence thou art fallen, and repent, and do the first works; or else I

*will come unto thee quickly, and will remove thy candlestick out of his place, except thou repent." Rev. 2: 4 - 5 **KJB***

I continued, "Today is the first day of the rest of your life if you want it to be, and it's your liberation day. No longer desolate, no longer bound. Let freedom ring!"

I cried with her as we shared, and I ministered. It was no accident that had that conversation. And we know that in all things, "*God works for the good of those who love him, who have been called according to his purpose." Romans 8:28 KJV*

Both shared with me how, if they were to confront their abusers or tell anyone, they would destroy and create a rift in the family. Revealing the truth must be God-inspired. I'm exposing my life because that is what God led me to do. It's not an easy subject or an easy place of revelation.

To those who face the same dilemma, I want to say that even if you never get a chance to confront your abusers, the healing must begin with you. Confronting them will not change the act, and most times, as in my case, they don't even believe that they did anything wrong. You must understand that their minds are warped to take advantage of a child in the first place. Therefore, anyone whose mind can so easily convince themselves to commit such an act is sick. It's not about the abuser; it's about overcoming. Even writing this book has been therapeutic and cathartic for me. My sincere prayer is that the guilty make recompense with their Maker, and if not, that God will have mercy on their souls. I reiterate; I'm Free. Let me take it a step further.

"Acceptance Speech"

As I stand and accept this Oscar for the leading role in "Behind the Collar," thank you to each of those who were the supporting actors in this film subtitled, "My Life."." Thank you for being the Catalysts who Catapulted me into my Calling. I couldn't have done it without you. (Holding up the bloodstained banner, throwing a kiss and bowing).

Frequently, sex serves as a means of escape, like crack to a crackhead. We try to make it our means of escape, but, it's the avenue to our bondage. The more sex we have, the better we think it will make us feel. We never really feel better. Every lay is another scar, on top of a scar. We keep chasing the thrill, but eventually, like B.B. King's song says,

"The Thrill is Gone." The void becomes deeper and deeper. It's all about broken trust, fear of rejection, and yearning for love. We chase and chase and chase after love, but it never comes. Instead, we need to be chasing after the Savior, and all other things will come.

"Delight yourself in the LORD, and he will give you the desires of your heart. Thank God for Jesus. There is nothing like the realization of His true and unconditional love." Psalms 37:4 NIV

God has made all the difference. He has proven to me repeatedly that He loves me more than anyone else, and He alone deserves my full loyalty, love, and affection.

I still have moments when I cry out as I think of my past, but today, my cries are different. They are not because I believe that I'm so bad, but because I know that God is so good. I can never be good enough to receive or be worthy of His mercy, but I receive His grace, and I feel good about Him.

"God's law was given so that all people could see how sinful they were. But as people sinned more and more, God's

wonderful grace became more abundant." Romans 5:20 NIV

He sacrificed all for such a worm as I. He died that I might live. He died and rose that I might die to my selfish wants and desires, and one day rise to be with Him throughout eternity.

I appeal to the hearts and minds of those who are reading this book. My life proves that He is a mind regulator and a heart fixer. God is a healer of broken hearts.

"He heals the brokenhearted and binds up their wounds." Psalms 147:3 NIV

I know this to be true because I am Healed! God is so awesome that the same thing He has done for me. He will do for you if you ask Him. The scars of molestation are deeply rooted, and the healing requires a deep uprooting and purging. While going through the process, the enemy takes you through a series of emotions, from feeling dirty, to unworthy, to unrecoverable. From the pits of hell, he is a liar, but I stand in solidarity with you, rebuking every one of these emotions in the name of JESUS. There are steps pertinent to your recovery:

Freedom must be something that you crave. No different than when you want some chocolate, and there is nothing that will satisfy that craving, but chocolate. You must thirst and hunger after righteousness. *"Blessed are those who hunger and thirst for righteousness, for they shall be filled." Matthew 5:6 KJV*

You must get under some anointed Word, a bible believing and teaching ministry. Ask God to send you to a place that has a deliverance ministry where they believe in ministering to the real issues that we face in life.

Stop and take a moment to pray this prayer with me:

Father God, in the name of Jesus, we first recognize you in all your glory and majesty. You are Jehovah Rapha, our healer, and you are Jehovah Mephalti, our deliverer. You are Jehovah Shalom, our peace, Jehovah Tsidkenu, our righteousness, and our strong tower. God touch all the places in me that are broken, damaged, and in that desolate place. Mend God, repair God, and revive, God. Restore me to you – my first love. Shower down your unconditional love. Reveal yourself in ways like never before. Help me to see me as you see me. Heal every fracture and mend every tear. Oh, God, heal, deliver, and set ME free. Remove not just the wounds, oh God, but erase the scars. Renew and revamp. In the name of Jesus. I speak it into the atmosphere, and I declare it so. In the name of Jesus, in the name of Jesus, in the matchless name of JESUS, the highest king. We shout - Hallelujah, Hallelujah, Hallelujah! We clap our hands, open our mouths, and seal it in the atmosphere through the blood that you shed on Calvary and counting it all done. Thank you, God, and Amen.

Wherever you are, lift your hands and tell God thank you. It's done. Hallelujah! It's done!

13

The Exordium: Beginning Again

I have waited for this seemingly a lifetime; my story is far too in-depth to tell it all,

God has been there every time; picking me up and dusting me off after every fall.

I'm here basking in this moment and bathing in God's eternal well.

As I rest here releasing the biggest breath, I can proclaim with assurance, I'm

No Longer Waiting ---- for in his arms, I now Exhale!

Two weeks before the birth of this book, I decided to rededicate and consecrate myself. I took my blessed oil and rubbed it on every part of my body from my head to my feet.

One week later, on September 17, 2012, God has me writing a book. Twelve days later, the outline of the book is finished – nobody but God.

As my niece says, "Where they do that at?"

To some, this may not seem like a big deal, but let me tell you what my current schedule was. I was in school, I worked two jobs, and I was involved in ministry. But, even if that were not the case, twelve days? That's fast, right?

The weeks after developing the book outline, remained crazy. I cried myself to sleep a few nights, not because I was sad, but because I was in awe of God and how gracious he had been to me, even while writing this book.

I have a jewel in my daughter Kianna. Let me tell you the profundity of it all. This is what had me torn up from the start. Ever since she was born, I prayed and prayed that her plight was not mine. As God often does, He gave me much more than requested.

"Now to him who can do immeasurably more than all we ask or imagine, according to his power that is at work within you." Ephesians 3:20 KJV

He kept my daughter naïve to all that I went through. She never saw the depth of my guilt, pain, anguish, low self-esteem, and brokenness. He gave me everything I needed to impart to her, all the things that I wasn't. He kept her innocent and put blinders on her eyes. She never saw me as anything but a woman of God. She saw me as God has now made me – whole, renewed, restored, strong, and holy; blameless and covered by the blood of Jesus. I'm fighting back the tears even now.

I had to do an assignment for school, and I chose "Abstinence" as a topic. I asked Ki-Ki if I could interview her. She agreed.

The last question in the interview was, "Why have you chosen to live a life of purity?"

She explained, "First off, it's because I'm a Christian, and the Bible states to wait until you are married. Secondly, I had a mother that raised me right. She taught me that I have value and worth; that I'm a queen."

I was a proud mother. I had further learned that she wants to start a worldwide crusade for girls about the importance of remaining pure. How glorious of God to extend his grace by allowing a broken vessel to produce seed. I'm so grateful and humbled by it all.

I was talking to her one Sunday morning, and she turned to me and said, "Mom, you couldn't have done a better job of raising me; you raised me perfectly."

What a mighty God we serve!

God deals with me in dreams and numbers. I love numbers and the revelations that are attached to them.

One night around 11:30-11:45, I had been in straight praise and thanksgiving for a while. God's unconditional love kept playing over and over in my mind. The more I thought about it, the more the tears began to flow, and the louder my cries got. God woke me up to write some things down that had been dropped in my spirit. He told me to look at the clock. It was midnight on the dot, and it was on the twenty-seventh of December. There was a common theme. It was 2012, the outline for the book took twelve days to write, and it's midnight in December, the twelfth month.

I had no idea that this was the common theme of this book the night before. The number twelve symbolizes God's perfect, divine accomplishment, actively manifested. JESUS! It shows the completeness of growth. Twelve marks governmental protection and is used as the signature of Israel (12 tribes). Twelve is the number for government by divine appointment, Hallelujah! God has perfected and appointed me for such a time as this.

Then, God, had me look up the number twenty-seven, which was the date and the beginning of the next day. I have a book that explains the meaning of numbers from a godly perspective. So, I turned to the number twenty-seven. I had written about a dream that God gave me a few years back that occurred on the twenty-seventh. I was bawling. I'm a big crybaby anyways, so it does not take much, at this point in my life, to make me cry tears of joy. The number twenty-seven is found a few times in the Bible. The number is made up of a combination of numbers that reveals the preaching of the gospel. I'm about to burst as I tell this to you.

In I Timothy 3:1-7, there are listed seventeen qualifications for the preacher of the gospel. Number seventeen is the number of victories. Bless your name, God! Number ten is the number for the law. Together, they give us the number twenty-seven. That attests to the fact that the preacher is one who gives his/her testimony of victory that the good news, the gospel, overcomes and frees from the law and gives victory to the life of the believer. Jesus, Jesus, Jesus. To God Be the Glory.

Every wound – healed.

Every scar – removed.

Every fingerprint – undetectable.

Every tear – mended.

I waited a long time for the ability to exhale. I was deceived into thinking that it was about waiting to exhale in the arms of a mortal man, but God had been waiting for me to exhale in the bosom of the holy man, Jesus. The wait is over. I'm No Longer Waiting to Exhale.

I named this chapter the same as the first because it's the end of the old creature and the beginning of the new. Old things are passed away and behold all things have become new. Welcome to the new me in Christ. *"Therefore, if anyone is in Christ, the new creation has come: The old has gone, the new is here!" II Corinthians 5:17 NIV.* Won't He do it?! My life has taken many dips and dives. It is my life and my story, but:

Out of All of This, God, You Get the Glory!

It's my past; it's my history,

But Mama, it's ok, because before I was formed in your belly,

He knew me, and before I came forth out of your womb, He sanctified me.

So, it's my history, but it's His story

And out of all this,

God, you, and you alone - Get All the Glory!

No Longer a Victim but a Victor!

14

The Exultation: Welcome to My Beginning

Free at last, Free at last!

Thank God almighty,

I'm Free at Last!

~ Reverend Martin Luther King, JR.

This joy I have, the world didn't give it, and the world can't take it away. Lord, have mercy!

I wrote this book in 2012. So, why didn't I release it before now? I have learned that just because God gave you something, doesn't mean that it's time to put it in motion. I had no idea at that time that he wasn't finished with the work in me. That was the beginning of the process.

2012 was the start of the healing process. I was forty-eight when things started to spiral uphill. I had joined New Zion Temple, not knowing that this place would be where I would recover.

As of this writing, I am fifty-five, and God told me this is the seventh year. 2012 to 2019 and forty-eight to fifty-five is seven years. The number seven represents the number of completion or perfection. I'm heading into number eight, a new beginning.

"But let patience have her perfect work, that ye may be perfect and entire, wanting nothing." James 1:4 KJV

Hallelujah! He told me that the cycle of my healing is now complete. When I tell you that revelation messed me up, it messed me up.

On January 13, 2019, I was on my way to a service where my daughter spoke. While driving, I declared this year; I would complete some things that had been lingering in the wings: the book and the release of my single.

The service had reached a high, and the prophet of the house started to speak over me.

He revealed, "Woman of God, there is a book in you. You have been procrastinating with finishing it. I see you doing book signings all over the world. What happened to you as a young child, God is giving you a clean slate. This book will cause some additional healing in you and help others heal as well."

I was completely floored and on the floor. It was amazingly unbelievable that he confirmed what I had mentioned on the drive.

God was still perfecting some things in me. There were some gifts that I had no idea lay dormant.

I was planning my big fiftieth birthday bash. As I was trying to decide what I wanted to do, it hit me, and I wanted to do a variety show with, me, as the star attraction. I only sing, so how will this play out. Unbeknownst to me, God had it all figured out. He started downloading characters into my spirit:

The Latin Lover - Maria Anna Consuela Cortez Hernandez Sanchez Smith

Reformed Pimp Uncle - Deacon PlayOn

Five-year-old – Kimora

The Stripper – Parkitta

Trailer Park Cousin – Carlotta

I called them "The Smiths." Their family history: Maria married into the Smith family. Her husband is Parkitta's brother. Deacon PlayOn is Parkitta's uncle. Parkitta is Kimora's mother, and Carlotta is their cousin. I walk around every day with six people in my head. At least mine are productive, and they keep me off medication.

I was fifty with my first one-person show. I danced, sang, introduced each character, and blew the crowd away. This was my Genesis. I was being reborn and metamorphosed into a new person, a new entity, the new, and improved *me*.

Like most people, I let the entire thing lay quiescent. Then, the Social Media era gained momentum. It finally hit me like a sledgehammer. I told myself, you need to start doing Facebook videos with the characters. I did just that! I'm still a little slothful with doing them frequently, but I'll do better.

In the spring of 2016, I told my daughter, "I'm going to be in somebody's play. I don't know when or how, but it's going to happen."

In the fall of 2016, I connected with a producer on Facebook, and by February 2017, I was on stage in my first real stage performance with PerSkription Entertainment entitled, "The Company You Keep."

Then the enemy tried to attack. In 2017, I was diagnosed with non-alcoholic fatty liver disease (NAFLD). That was anomalous to me because I am active in the gym, and I ate healthy foods most of the time. I started researching and taking natural things that I thought could assist in at least keeping it stable to no avail.

In March 2018, I went to the doctor and got a negative report. I knew that it was the NAFLD, but what could I do. A friend told me about Black Seed Oil. I had never heard of it, but I did my research by reading peer-reviewed studies about it. You always want to read articles where there have been actual studies on it with conclusive evidence to support the findings. Don't read or trust websites called Mike's Monthly Medical Murmurings. I took it for three months and then went back to the doctor. There was absolutely no evidence of the disease. God did that thang!

My life has been a nightmare and a fairytale all in one. Last year was more than surreal.

In 2018, at the tender age of fifty-four I:

- Launched my Facebook Page – Special Ks Komedy Korner
- YouTube Channel – Special Ks Komedy Korner
- Became Praise and Worship leader at Cathedral of Joy
- Was Healed from NAFLD
- Won a forty-inch-inch flat screen TV
- Performed in two comedy shows with Big Keef and Just Nesh.
- Won airline tickets
- Graduated with a Master of Science in Sports nutrition with a 4.0 g.p.a.

While on this journey, I also:

- Earned an Associate of Applied Science in Fitness and Exercise with honors
- Earned a Bachelor of Science in Sports Medicine - Magna Cum Laude.
- Performed in two plays

I have five plays under my belt and looking to do more.

In 2019 I:

- Have several confirmed contracts to perform comedy
- Finishing this book
- Filming for a pilot show
- On the radio - 88.7 FM - Gary - "Wellness Wednesday."
- Have several singing engagements and stand up comedy gigs.
- Working on completing my single entitled, *I Surrender All.*

I could not have written a better script for my life at this moment in time, but I realize that it's the Lord's doing and it's marvelous in His eyes. He is the author and producer. He wrote the storyline before the foundation of the world, and I'm playing my part by actively fulfilling my role.

I am fifty-five and thus entering a year of double favor, not to mention the senior discounts that have been more than a blessing thus far. I'm getting all that God has for me. I'm not going to stop. I gotta, Get It, Get It!

I present to some and introduce to others: The preacher, teacher, singer, songwriter, comedian, actress, poet, teacher, fashionista, and now an author.

Watch me work!

15

The Extremity: The Wrap Up

Even though my ministry relates more to women, some men suffer from the scars of molestation. As mentioned previously, I had the opportunity to minister to a young man who was struggling with his sexuality due to his experience with molestation. I couldn't identify with his struggle, but I did understand the root of it. I hope the men who read it gain a better understanding of themselves and perhaps the behavior associated with it, whatever it may be and seek God for healing. Not only that, but I also pray men will gain better insight into women that suffer or have suffered from this abuse.

Even though therapy was not something that I pursued, I am a proponent of it. Seeking help does not imply that you are crazy; it says that you are courageous. Asking for help suggests that you will not allow fear and the opinions of others to immobilize and keep you from becoming whole. I suffered the entire time in silence, and I wonder if perhaps my healing would've been expedited if therapy was used in tandem with the natural process. One can't know for sure, but it's something I would suggest. Seek out a therapist that has experience in dealing with molestation. Additionally, speak with a person who has overcome it. Nothing better than hearing someone else's testimony of victory.

The triangle was portrayed throughout the book repeatedly:

<u>Manipulation</u> is all about control. Once a person can control your view of yourself, they can control your thoughts about yourself and your actions. Men who are predators feed off weakness. No different than a wolf that preys on rodents. Instinctually and inherently, it's what they do. These men are ruthless and are good at exploitation. Rest assured, in the end, all predators become the prey.

"I will take revenge; I will pay them back," says the Lord. Romans 12:19 NLT

God sees all things, and you cannot be so arrogant as to think that when you mistreat people, there will be no justice.

All deviants shall suffer by God's hand; I pray that God is merciful.

Sex addiction is no different than drug addiction, and according to the word of God, it's a major offense against the body.

"18. Flee fornication. Every sin that a man doeth is without the body, but he that committeth fornication sinneth against his own body. 19. What? Know ye not that your body is the temple of the Holy Ghost, which is in you, which ye have of God, and ye are not your own? 20. For ye are bought with a price: therefore, glorify God in your body, and in your spirit, which is God's." I Corinthians 6:18-20 KJV

Even deeper is the tie, connection, and bond created that sometimes is the greatest stronghold imaginable. It's deeply rooted at times that you become a junky, dependent upon it. Your body goes through withdrawals.

You ever wonder why you are calling him obsessively and stalking him, depressed and looking through his phone? Or seeing who he's currently dating on Facebook and Instagram? It's because they transfer their issues, demons, and the demons of others they have been with to you. Sex was what trapped me and kept me bound to it for years. I thought if I sexed them well, that was enough to keep them. It has the same effect as any other ad(dick)tion, but this one, only God can break.

<u>Rejection</u> is often internalized and taken personally. When you suffer from it, you start asking repetitive questions like What is wrong with me? Why am I not good enough? Why doesn't he see that I am a good person? All these questions become legitimized, in your mind, when you're broken and oblivious to your worth. The only way to recover is through God's validation. You must see yourself how he sees you. You must love yourself as he loves you. Then and only then will you begin to see the queen or king that he created you to be. When you do, it's as if scales have been removed from your inner core. It's a rebirth, like a transformation from the old to the new you. It's the end of a vicious cycle of self-doubt and self-lambasting. It's an awakening from a place you never want to revisit again, EVER.

Manipulation, sex, and rejection were the roots of my brokenness. They resonated loud and clear in every relationship, in some form. I was an obsequious servant to them all. Singly they caused brokenness, but as unit, dictated the fragments of my life like broken glass. Unlike all the king's horses and all the king's men who couldn't put Humpty Dumpty back together again, I know the King of Kings and the Lord of Lords, who mended every fragment and every tear. He is an amazing God!

The daily struggle is real. The sex demons hunt me no differently than any other issues that people face. I will not lie and say that I have not slipped or fallen off the wagon since the beginning of this process. I have, and more than once. I am not glorying or reveling in it at all. I want it known that I have issues like everyone else. However, I can promise that I do not participate in habitual sin. More importantly, God's grace has been enough for me, and I thank Him for it every day. Believe that!

This book is meant to shine a light, not on an individual, but the sin and the behavior resulting from it. I have come full circle with it all, and I'm not angry with anyone. All the scenarios were presented to you as if it were in real-time. They expressed my thoughts and feelings as they occurred at those moments. To all the super deep saints, continue to drown in the shallow waters, if you will. I care not what you feel or think. This book is about helping others understand that they are not alone. I wish you Grace and Peace.

I have reconciled with some of the people described in this book, but for those I haven't, well, peace be with them because for me: All Is Well!

I hope that you enjoyed the snippets of my poetry sprinkled throughout my story. I have included a "For Your Entertainment" section that contains each poem in its entirety plus a few of my favorites. Turn on some soft music, get a glass of wine, (lighten up saints), and ride with me into some of my moments of expression.

For Your Entertainment: Expressions for your pleasure
I Am Not the One

I realize things can't always be understood,
There is sometimes no rhyme or reason for what should, would or could.

I realize that no matter what you might want or think is to be,
Makes no difference, for if the agendas are different, that changes the reality.

I have come to the awareness that one can't predict the actions of another,
For people are good at wearing facades & disguises, and work well undercover.

Amid learning & growth to such a high degree,
I can't accept many things, and there are many things, with which I don't agree.

I know that I'm not alone feeling as if I'm in the lion's lair,

Looking for a place of refuge, an avenue marked "fair."

Well, I can see clearly that a new life has begun,
And I see even clearer that I'm not the one.

I'm not the one, whom he reaches out to in the middle of the night,
I'm not the one who has constancy in his eyesight.

I'm not the one who has the luxury and comfort of his life,
For often, I feel myself holding on to hopeless dreams with all my might.

I'm not the one with the keys to the palace,
I'm but an outcast full of discontent and solace.

I'm to blame for what I have been a party to,
It's what I have accepted to be the truth and nothing but the truth.

Now I must reevaluate the current state of affairs,
Focus on the fate of my life and becoming even more aware.

The time has now arrived where the final chapter has been written.
Let go of what saddens me and allow healing to begin.

I'm standing here witnessing this affair and trying
to swallow the fact that his heart, she has won,

I can wish all day long, and as hard as it is to fathom,
I must accept that; I'm Not the One.

You Just Don't Understand

There is a spiritual order to God's creation and the way it's devised,
He made the man to be the head of the relationship and not the behind.

He is to love the woman and make her feel secure,
If he is negligible in any of these things, it makes the woman unsure.

Unsure if she can trust him with undying honor and respect,
If she does not, it brings about a crushing sense of neglect.

He is to build her up where she is torn down
and make her feel that all is right,
He is to be a reflection of her in view and even out of sight.

He must understand that he is only as strong as his woman and she only as strong as he,
But it starts at the top and trickles down from the Master of immortality.

If my man does not build up in me, my self-worth day by day,
If my love runs deep, it's inevitable the pain will forever stay.

Stay as a reminder of what I never want to feel again,
That is the pain, which can only come, from putting my trust and faith in a man.

Not a Good Place to Be!

I have found myself today to be where I thought I would never again have a front seat,
I feel like just giving up on love, for it just keeps bringing me to defeat.

I find myself wondering, "Why do I have to continue to feel this pain?"
I have made amends with a pure heart, but the wounds remain.

I find myself asking questions that I can't find answers to,
I'm playing them over and over in my mind, and I just don't know what to do.

Oh Lord, I need your help to carry me from this season in my life,
I can't do it alone because everything is as dark as night.

I find myself not knowing what I should feel, when, and how,

I have got to find a place of tranquility in all this, and I really need it now.

I find myself feeling like a fool, putting everything I have on the table,
I guess this is the time to trust in you completely and know that you are able.

Able to mend the broken pieces of my hurting heart,
You will not put more on me than I can bear; you will not allow me to fall apart.

I'm told that I'm not consistent, yet inconsistency is thrown at me on every turn,
I started to rest in what was told to me, and now for me, he no longer yearns.

Please help me God out of this place full of woe and despair,
I really am sincere about this thing, but how do I convey to him how much I really care?

He is supposed to be the covering in my life, a place of refuge by which I can find placidity,
Yet I feel abandoned and uncovered, as in a line, blind folded with my back towards the enemy.

Well, Lord, it's now all in your hands, whatever you want to do I give it all to thee,
Remove these chains of bondage, Lord; I want to again be free.

Free to feel, free to dance, free to love and be one in the institution you have decreed for humanity,
But right now, where I am is Not A Good Place to Be!

The Last Refrain

Sitting here pondering how blissful things used to be,
My heart cries out, praying that will not be our destiny.

I can't put my finger on what has happened to take us to this place of insecurity,
How can we change this? Is there something we can do or something we can say?

I'm willing to change and right all the wrong that's been done,
If you can find it in your heart to forgive me and help untangle the web that's been spun.

I genuinely love you, and I will give you all that you could want and desire,
You must first free yourself from all old memories and let me take you where there is no expire.

Believe that life is what you make it, and all is here to enjoy,
Know that what I tell you I feel is real, and not some disguised decoy.

Let me love you, and be in your world the missing link,
The link that holds our love together and brings our souls in sync.

I promise and vow to you my unconditional
and undying love,
A true love that is for you only and blessed by Heaven up above.

Things will be better if you tell yourself they will,
If you remove the wall of Berlin, and in the storm be still.

I can't express to you on paper the magnitude of my bond to you,
However, I can prove my sincerity in everything I say and do.

Each second, each moment, and each day
that passes, my love will tell,
Just know that I'm here for you in every way, no matter what it entails.

Be my love forever, and forever my love will remain,
Even until the end of time and when the music reaches its
Last Refrain.

Who Knew?

As the video played and things started to pass through my mind,
There was an overpowering stirring of no other kind.

I tried to go back to events and circumstances through reflection,
But where I found myself was in the present and contemplation.

I was in a reverie state, and bliss-filled my being,
Not fully understanding what I was feeling or seeing.
Then it hit as if the world had fallen from its axis,
Jarring me and tossing me into different factions.

I began to realize that my life has now become euphoric,
As it became clearer, there was no ambivalence that truly
You are the source.

I can't even begin to expound on this turn of events,
All I can extrapolate from it is that's what was meant.

This has overwhelmed me in more ways than I could ever imagine,
You have completed me and made me feel things that have no origin.

There is a new year rapidly approaching, waiting for no one,
We must grab hold of its trail, reaching heights and depths in our own private symposium.

I can express that I now know what it feels like for your soul to have a mate,
It's beyond anything that I could've conceived,
For its meaning, from my mind, has found an escape.

You have taken me to a realm that is beyond comprehension,
What we can reach together has its own undefined dimension.

Where we were, where we are, where we shall be,
Has been and will continue to be totally dictated by God, you, and me.

You can trust me and relax; I'm here to fulfill all your desires,
I will be the stimulus that leads you to new places, soaring higher and higher.

When I think about us and what all we have collectively been through,
All I can say is, Wow, this is awesome – and this right now, right here, Who Knew?

Broken I Am

Man, this is deep and truly a reality check,
I have thought to myself all I have done was
from the heart, what the heck!

I question, how important have I been or how significant is what we have shared?
Has it not mattered that I have given all that I could give; do you even care?

Poem after poem, expression after expression, things from the innermost depths of my soul,
Trying to reveal to you just how vital you are to me without, apparently, any console.

You don't even think before you speak; whatever you conceive is what flows from your tongue,
This is an old song that I wish was unsung.

I feel like I'm not the one that you professed you'd hold dear or in a special place in your life,

You made a choice; stood before God and man and swore to treat me as your wife.
Are my feelings hurt in a manner that one can't begin to imagine?
Yes, it's of such magnitude that I feel masticated and ripped from within.

I'm torn in a way that is incomprehensible to even me,
I gave you the richest, deepest, and uttermost
part that could ever be.

My heart has been reserved for you and only you,
Can you say the same of me; would that be the truth?

The tears are flowing now intensely as does blood from a punctured artery,
Trying to be strong for my girls but they are coming uncontrollably.

As I press through and attempt to regroup from what seems like a continuous heart spasm,
I must confess, if never again, right now, Broken I Am.

Pain

Pain carries a multitude of elements that penetrate you to the core,
Pain will make you shut, not just every window but close every door.

Pain will cause you to lose all faith and hope,
Pain is like a drug addict that fiends for some dope.

Pain stretches and carries every emotion
into a desolate place,
Pain is one of those things that is virtually impossible to erase.

If this is what I must endure even to love again,
I'll pass, this is some bull, for loving on a man.

I'm tired of withdrawals from my love account,
Tired of begging and pleading for one deposit of just a menial amount.

Pain trivializes the true meaning of love and what it's meant to be,
I know God created woman for man, but this thing is full of calamity.

Forget it, forget them all, for me, time is on the horizon,
Ready him for me, God, and help him see that even with all my flaws - without a doubt - I'm the one.

His missing rib, his friend, his lover, his mate,
Help him to know that upon my breastbone, his head can lie and be sedate.

God, I pray this is not my daughter's plight when love approaches her life,
I don't want her to feel this grief, for this cuts deeper than the sharpest knife.

I will endure this if I must to secure her fate,
Get him ready for her, Lord, the perfect one, her soul mate.

I will wait if I must even though it's the hardest strain,

In the interim, God, please release me from this heartache, from this excruciating PAIN.

Independence Day

I feel like I'm a ball in a tennis match, missing the ball but constantly and consistently trying,
Now coming to the realization that instead of him, it was God I should've been eying.

God, what did I do to deserve such disgrace?
I prayed to you and prayed to you earnestly desiring a mate.
I gave him all my heart, my mind, body, and soul...
I guess in retrospect; I gave him way too much control.

Man, but I was supposed to be the one who he loved and cared about more than any other,
But he treated me like less than a human being; I believe he chose over me, another.

I'm knocking at the door, trying to get in
and be with my man,
He entered inside me two days before, and then two days later, he's with another woman?

How could this happen, oh man of God that he "professes" to be?
He has made a mockery of God, His Word, and our unity.

Well, I find consolation in knowing that every dog has his day,
God will pass His judgment and vengeance upon him in a mighty way.

Even in this hurt, I pray for his soul and that God has mercy when He brings down His wrath,
Prayerfully, he will see the error of his ways and ask God to show him the right path.

Well, one thing that I'm now glorying in is that emancipation is right around the corner,
God is so awesome that when He frees you, there is nothing left to wonder.

Miracles are in His hands and His power is beyond all imaginable,
I'm giving it to God to redo me and make me again whole.

But now I see things for what they really are,

Yes, I'm wounded, and yes, I do now have a scar.
The scar will fade in time, though, and the memory will become faint,
I will look back on this and realize it helped me secure my fate.

This too shall pass, and going forward
I will never forget Jan. 5, 2008.
For this was the day that God released me
from the baggage, this was my Independence Day!

Yet Again

Yet again I find my heart filled with
grief and despair,
I surely thought this time around would
be just and fair.

Yet again I'm wondering if I will ever find
that true love,
A love that will encompass every part of
me and be as serene as a dove.

Yet again I'm in a place that reeks of
disharmony and dysfunction,
The questions keep coming and coming causing quite a bit
of internal commotion.

Yet again I find myself trying to be strong but constantly
fighting back the tears,
Tears of great pain and sorrow that
seem never to disappear.

Yet again I see myself struggling to arrest in my mind, the endless nights that are sure to come,
Will there ever be an end to this story because it feels like I've only just begun.

Yet again, I hope and pray that this will not last,
However, I'm on constant rewind, ruminating on the present and the past.

Yet again I think why me, why can't I find a place of solitude amid this storm,
Someplace that will shield me, cover me,
keep me safe and warm?

Well yet again, I must start over and, through God, rebuild all that has been lost,
I entered this without adding up the cost.

Yet again, here I am...damn, damn, damn.

Amend

I try to be strong through my sometimes-apparent weakness,
I fast and pray, pray, and fast, and still, events past and present overcome me like a sickness.

A sickness that penetrates my entire being physically and emotionally,
That I just ache, and ache, toil and toil and realize that this is for real, truly.

I have so much to give and yet no one to give it to,
The ones whom I've allowed to reach my soul have pierced it until it's black and blue.

Why I ask, why, Lord, have so much grief and distress come my way?
Have I erred so badly in the past that I have been deemed this level of calamity?

I'm so tired and weary, trying, Lord, to stay within Your will,
I have been listening earnestly for a word, but to clearly hear, perhaps I haven't really stood still.

Please heal my broken heart and bind up my wounds that lie so deep within,
I thought that I would never have to cross this path again.

To my surprise, my life keeps on, in some ways, repeating itself,
Even when I think I've hidden my feelings and placed them securely on a high shelf.

They somehow find their way off, and again the circle of life has taken control,
Lord, may I please call a time out for you to wipe the slate clean and make me whole?

Complete me in a way that I have never been,
So, I can easily see when one's true personality is not a disguise of sin.

I'm trying to have the faith and trust in you for what I need,
But I'm at a weak point in my life, and sometimes I just can't seem to breathe.

I feel stagnated and broken, trying to move and mend,
I'm frozen by the many emotions that I have;
fear is conquering me, and I know not where to begin.

I need you right now currently and, in this place,
Please fill the void in this huge and lonely, empty space.

I know that only you love me unconditionally and cherish me for the gift that I am,

This, too, shall pass, and all that the enemy meant to steal, kill, and destroy, you will restore, renew, and Amend.

Tired!

Trying to find a place of comfort in this tumultuous whirlwind,
Don't know where to start, no clue on where to begin.

Want to be "in like" for love is easy to achieve,
I'm standing at the starting line, counting in disbelief.

I feel as if my body has been placed in stasis,
Am I waiting to be revived and then forced back to the basics?

What perplexes me about it all is that it's hard to remain sane,
It feels like electric shocks are flowing through every ventricle, every vein.

I know I will recover as in other times before,
The difference is I want to throw away the key this time and stand behind the locked door.

My heart is telling me, "You will heal, and you will feel again."
To not have faith is very much a tragic sin.

Knowing this, I will press on; towards the mark, I will aspire. But man, when I think about it all, mentally and emotionally, I'm just plain Tired.

To Thee

I'm resting here at my desk, feeling things that have overtaken me and subdued me in ways unimaginable,
I wish I could touch you, see you, walk with you, but you are not physically tangible.

Trying to swallow the tears every second as I write these words on paper,
Caught up in a tunnel of expression; realizing that you are my redeemer, healer, and keeper.

Each and everything that is coming now to my mind is making my tears harder and harder to hold back,
I'm so grateful for everything in my life, good, indifferent, and even more when there was lack.

You have been there in times that I wanted just to give up and throw in the towel,
Meekly as a lamb, I'm here before you, all to you I give, and I humbly bow.

My heart is filled with great ebullience, more than I can bear,
To know that there is someone that would give all for me, someone that could as much – even care.

I'm so unworthy of such an honor, so unworthy of the blessings and even more, all the undeserved favor,
There is nothing I can do to repay you, but I will serve you because you have truly been my Savior.

I can't seem to fathom anything for what you have given is of such magnitude,
Without you being so prevalent in my life, I don't know where I would be or what I would do.

Tears are now streaming down the sides of each one of my cheeks,
I'm not concerned about who may walk by or who might be privy to see.

If I'm asked, I will just simply tell them that, "All that I am, and all that I could ever hope to be,"

Oh God, my Lord, and my King, I owe it all unto none other than Unto Thee!

"I Never Knew" (Original song lyrics)

I never knew someone would love me so deeply,
To look beyond all my faults and love me completely.

I never knew I could have a love to call my own,
That would bring me such peace and I'd never again be alone.

I never knew I could have joy inside of tears,
That would ease the pain and relieve all my doubts and all my fears.

Lord, you made the difference

I never knew, someone willing to give their life
for me
Who would give everything He had so I could live with Him throughout eternity?

I never knew I'd find a man such as this,
That his blood would cleanse my soul and all my sins He would remit.

But I found someone who loves me for me just for me.
I found someone who cares for me – Lord, I found you.
He gave everything for me.
Lord, you made the difference.

No Longer Waiting to Exhale

Last night I was taken on a ride,
It wasn't as a merry-go-round going in circles but as a riptide.

It swept through my soul and titillated my senses,
It was like the final speech given at a graduation commencement.

It inspired and lifted me like no other experience,
It filled me with joy, love, and hope; it truly showed me the difference.

The difference between hearing mere words and filling one's heart,
It overcame and satiated me; there wasn't anything carnal about it; it was dreamlike from the start.

As many times as I've watched the movie, and heard the phrase repeatedly,
The true definition of love had somehow gotten past me.

As I lay in my bed crying, praising, and luxuriating every second of every moment,
Time rushed past as you sang me a love song and made me feel oh so content.

You've challenged me to expose myself, and you see me in ways no other really has,
It's all good, though, because, with you, there is comfort, refuge, and direction, as a compass.

Being with you relaxes me, soothes me, and takes my breath away,
Each moment with you is synonymous with the blessing of a new day.

When you first held me in your arms, there was a calming that enamored me,
All the things that were once in my mind a fantasy seemed to now be a reality.

It's now apparent to me what "Waiting to Exhale" means,
It's anomalistic in nature and as of another galaxy.

This time has been well spent, and I recognize it for the gift that it is,
I'm nervously waiting with anticipation like the spontaneity and anxiety of a pop quiz.

I have waited for this seemingly a lifetime; my story is far too in-depth to tell it all,
God has been there every time; picking me up and dusting me off after every fall.

I'm here basking in this moment and bathing in God's eternal well.
As I rest here releasing the biggest breath, I can proclaim with assurance, I'm No Longer Waiting ---- for in his arms, I now Exhale!

Out of All of This, God, You Get the Glory!

He was slick and sly, fine, and fly; slithered his way in,
Caused me to stumble & fall time after time into more and more sin.

When I was 12, he showed up and violated my trust,
It made my body feel things a normal adolescent shouldn't feel; I remember trying to make sense of it all and adjust.

Feeling like Oprah from "The Color Purple," all my life I've had to fight,
Fight the sexual demons that still haunt and taunt me morning, noon, and night.

Made me abort that king or queen that was growing in my womb,
But I loved him oh so much, my heart, my mind, my soul he had consumed.

Now I'm so smitten, totally taken by the master mathematician who can take 1+1+1 make it divisible unto itself and = 1,

The one who concluded that the definition of love would be the giving of his only begotten son.

Not another man shall deposit himself into me and withdraw snippets of my soul,
For God has remolded me as does a potter with clay, reconstructed me, and now I'm whole.

God, now I boldly proclaim you as my judge and I as your witness,
And as the gavel hits the wood, your blood has erased the guilty stain affirmed and reaffirmed my innocence.

Now if by chance you were in wonderment as to why I worship and praise Him as I do,
Look at me. I'm not the ugly sweater at Christmas re-gifted,
I now present myself, presently, brand spanking new.

Now the tears I shed are no longer tears of sorrow and despair,
Only God could've kept me from breaking and shattering into pieces, I know for myself He cares.

Yes, my life was all messed up, flipped over and shipwrecked,
How you like me now, I look good, feel good, I'm good,
Satan - thought it time to give you a reality check.

You can't hold a good woman, oh,
excuse me, I mean a God woman, down,
We are as black diamonds, rare and not easily found.

He should've killed me when I wanted to die, medicated, and sedated me when I was depressed.
It's too late now, baby because I'm free
and now I place you Satan under arrest.

I've been broken, beaten, battered, bruised, and berated,
Now I'm restored, revamped, renewed, revived, redeemed, and rejuvenated.

Told me repeatedly, no one will ever love you, you should just kill yourself and die,
How many of you know He can have back that Hallmark card from the pits of hell because that's a multi-colored lie.

For now, I know who loved me when I didn't even love myself,
Who rescued me when I had not sense enough to cry for help?

It's my past; it's my history,
But Mama, it's ok, because before I was formed in your belly,
He knew me, and before I came forth out of your womb,
He sanctified me.

So, it's my history, but it's His story
And out of all this, out of all this,
God, you, and you alone - Get All the Glory!

Dedication: Ode to Kiki

I find myself faced with a great dilemma that I can't seem to explain,
I keep searching and searching for answers that will make things clear and plain.

I have reflected and replayed the question repeatedly and addressed it to people of all,
Still, there is no resolve to the mystery; from mankind of great stature and of small.

Why, why, why must it be this way?
Why must it be sunny and bright on one shore, but on another, cloudy, dark, and gray?

What makes the sand be blinding in its natural state?
But pressed and refined can enable clearer sight to men of old and slow gait.

Has the sin of our forefathers not made us endure enough calamity?
That it must go on and on throughout all of humanity?

What do I tell my daughter about the state that things are in?
How do I save her from the great unforeseen but inevitable whirlwind?

How can I keep her from experiencing all the pain, hurt, and grief?
Will my words ever be comforting enough to soothe and give her relief?

I dare to think that she is faced with even more than my life has brought,
Even though I have searched for outlets and true love readily sought.

I do have the one and only solution to her finding her place,
It alone lies in God to lead and guide her to her own private space.

I know that if I can convince her to rely on and trust in Him for totality,
Some things that were dreams for me will be her reality.

She will grow up with virtue, knowledge, and power that will carry her through the darkness,
She will, inconstancy, seek God's face, and feel His omnipresence.

She will not have to answer the questions that have for so long befuddled me,
For to her, they will be apparent and made plain through God and His divinity.

She will have the love that I have forever been in search of,
For her there will be no exploration; she will receive it as a gift that can only come from God above.

What I Want / What I Need

What I want is my best friend,
What I need is for him to prove to be such and not just a pretense.

What I want is to be able to rest in the vow that was made,
What I need is for the vow to be taken seriously enough to dispel the charade.

What I want is to be with him all by my own choice.
What I need is not to hear the words spoken but to feel the inner voice.

What I want is to know that I can trust him completely.
What I need is not to be judged by my uncertainty.

What I want is not to have to perform mental gymnastics and always guess.
What I need is to simplify things, and it is no game of chess.

What I want is to feel protected beyond all measure.

What I need is to be polished and covered as if of the finest treasure.
What I want is all about redefining the things that we say are complicated into facile form,
What I need is not to be presented with signs, wonders, and geometric equations
that are way beyond the norm.

If I could just instill some understanding into the ignorance that apparently resounds so definitively,
It would be all good because then not only would I have What I Want, I would get What I need!

When

When will you surrender and give yourself to me?
When will you allow your heart, mind, and spirit to be free?

When will you allow me to inundate you with the aroma of my essence?
When will you allow my love to become a permanent part of your presence?

When will your love for me become solidified?
When will you allow my love to within you rest, rule, and abide?

I will not make excuses or apologize for my tenacity,
It's you who has my heart in bondage; you have put me in captivity.

You have been the experience that I never imagined I would receive,
You have taught and shown me things that have permeated my mind and are sure never to leave.

You will one day realize the precious gift that you have been sent,
If you would give me that part of you that has for so long been in torment.

I know that things are good, but I could surely make them better,
I would be the missing piece of the puzzle that holds your life together.

For I am a woman, the perfect specimen, custom made especially for you,
I'm gentile but strong, graceful as a swan, intelligent, sensitive, and true.

You and you alone possess the same tailor-made design,
You are tender but mighty, spirited as a steed, sagacious, sexy, and genuine.

We are the pattern; the blueprint of a well-sculpted masterpiece,

We are the foundation and geographic border of an architectural release.
Let's start from the beginning and make all that is old renewed,
Let's blend it all together with a love that could never be consumed.

We are the author and editor of our own destiny,
We can write the storyline; we can make it a reality.

I can't continue this path of uncertainty for it has no compare,
I need to know what you are feeling, how much you genuinely care.

So again, I ask, "When will you surrender yourself to me,"
"When will you allow your heart, mind, and spirit to be free?"

I hope that you enjoyed excerpts from "Poems from the Heart." Let me know if you did. They were my way of sharing my private thoughts and heart with you.

I look forward to hearing your comments about and responses to the book as well. I will read them and respond.

I thank you, in advance, for your support.

Much love and many blessings to you forever.

I wish you Grace and Peace!

Made in the USA
Monee, IL
25 September 2022